TROTMAN

Trotman careers titles are available from all good bookshops or can be ordered direct from:	Bailey Distribution Ltd Learoyd Road Mountfield Road Industrial Estate New Romney Kent TN28 8XU Tel: 01797 369961 Fax: 01797 366638

This sixth edition published in 1998 in Great Britain by
Trotman & Company Ltd,
12 Hill Rise, Richmond, Surrey TW10 6UA

British Library Cataloguing in Publication Data
A catalogue record for this book is available from the British Library

ISBN 0 85660 362 7

Printed and bound in Great Britain

CONTENTS

ABOUT THE AUTHOR

Alan Vincent graduated with a French degree from Reading University in 1964. After teaching in Nigeria and Hertfordshire, he became Head of Guidance and Admissions for the North Oxfordshire Centre of Advanced Studies and then TVEI Coordinator for North Oxfordshire. Since 1994 he has been self-employed as a consultant, with a core contract as the Coordinator for the North Oxfordshire Learning Partnership and Manager of the local Education Business Partnership.

Alan has been a member of the Executive Council of the National Association of Careers and Guidance Teachers (NACGT) since 1976. He was General Secretary from 1979 to 1984 and President from 1985 to 1987. Throughout his career he has made significant contributions to the development of careers education and guidance, for example through his involvement in training courses run by NACGT, ICG, CRAC, NAPCE, LEAs and TECs.

GLOSSARY OF ABBREVIATIONS

ACAC	Curriculum & Assessment Authority for Wales
A-level	Advanced Level
AS-level	Advanced Supplementary/Subsidiary Level
ASDAN	Award Scheme Development & Accreditation Network (Youth Award Scheme)
BA	Bachelor of Arts degree
BSc	Bachelor of Science degree
BTEC	Business & Technology Education Council (now Edexcel Foundation)
CCEA	Council for the Curriculum, Examinations & Assessment (Northern Ireland)
CDT	Craft, Design & Technology
CLCI	Careers Library Classification Index
CRAC	Careers Research & Advisory Centre
CSYS	Certificate of Sixth Year Studies (Scotland)
DENI	Department of Education for Northern Ireland
DfEE	Department for Education & Employment
GCSE	General Certificate of Secondary Education
GNVQ	General National Vocational Qualification
GOML	Graded Objective in Modern Languages
GRC	Grade Related Criteria (Scotland)
GSVQ	General Scottish Vocational Qualification
H Grade	Higher Grade (Scotland)
HMI	Her Majesty's Inspectorate
HNC	Higher National Certificate
HND	Higher National Diploma
ICG	Institute of Careers Guidance
IT	Information Technology
KS	Key Stage
LEA	Local Education Authority
LCCI	London Chamber of Commerce & Industry
MEG	Midland Examining Group
NACGT	National Association of Careers & Guidance Teachers
NAPCE	National Association for Pastoral Care in Education
NEAB	Northern Examinations & Assessment Board
NC	National Curriculum
NCVQ	National Council for Vocational Qualifications

NNEB	National Nursery Examination Board
NVQ	National Vocational Qualification
OFSTED	Office for Standards in Education
PSE	Personal & Social Education
QCA	Qualifications & Curriculum Authority
RSA	Royal Society of Arts
S Grade	Standard Grade (Scotland)
SCAA	School Curriculum & Assessment Authority
SCCC	Scottish Consultative Council on the Curriculum
SCOTVEC	Scottish Vocational Education Council
SCE	Scottish Certificate of Education
SEG	Southern Examining Group
SQA	Scottish Qualifications Authority
SVQ	Scottish Vocational Qualification
TEC	Training & Enterprise Council
TVEI	Technical & Vocational Education Initiative
UCAS	Universities & Colleges Admissions Service
WJEC	Welsh Joint Education Committee

1. GETTING THE FACTS STRAIGHT

The GCSE countdown has now begun. What are you letting yourself in for? Let's begin by getting a few of the facts straight.

What is the GCSE?

GCSE stands for General Certificate of Secondary Education.

Who is the GCSE for?

YOU. It is designed as a two-year course of study for students in Years 10 and 11 (Years 11 and 12 in Northern Ireland).

At Key Stage 4 (KS4) GCSE is the main means of assessing attainment. New criteria for GCSE examinations are in line with the revised National Curriculum which is now fully in place at KS4.

Can everybody take the GCSE?

Yes. The GCSE is open to anyone who can meet its requirements, regardless of their age or circumstances of study. The GCSE is therefore available to both mature and private candidates as well as all those in schools and colleges.

When do I take the exam?

The usual age to sit the end-of-course exam is 16... but there are no hard and fast rules. You can take it before or after that age.

There is some more information about taking the GCSE early and its implications in the next chapter – GCSE and the National Curriculum.

When can I sit the exam?

There are two sittings each year. Most students will sit the exam in the Summer when all subjects are on offer. In most subjects, the exams are held in May/June. The second sitting is in either November or January, depending on what course you are taking. Not all subjects are offered in these Autumn or Winter examinations.

Why do I need to take the GCSE?

Sixteen is a turning point in every young person's life. It is a time of change. Some of you may leave school and take a job or start on a training placement. Most of you will stay on in full-time education, at either school or college, for at least one or two more years, in order to improve your range of skills and qualifications. For some the aim will be to take further examinations, like A-levels or a General National Vocational Qualification (GNVQ), and perhaps go on to university or a college of higher education.

For all, GCSE offers an opportunity to assess your skills and abilities and help you decide how you can improve these and use them to direct you along more specific lines.

What makes the GCSE different from examinations in the past?

GCSE is designed to relate to young people's everyday lives. For example, syllabuses address economic, political, social and environmental matters, where these are appropriate and relevant to the particular subject. They also provide opportunities for the appropriate use of Information Technology, to complement and reinforce work done in that particular subject.

With the GCSE, there is more emphasis on problem solving and using the knowledge you have gained. That is why GCSE courses include practical work, oral work, fieldwork, investigations, projects, even group work. The result is that courses are more interesting, more inventive and more useful. It all means less time being a passive learner and more time spent on projects, problem solving and finding out for yourself.

Most GCSEs include coursework – that's work you do during the two years. And the marks for your coursework count towards your final result. Exams are fine for testing knowledge and, to some extent, understanding. But they favour people with a good memory and there are many skills which an exam can't test at all. How, for example, can an exam show how good you are at looking up information and using it? Or at carrying out your own project? The GCSE format will not only test your knowledge of formulae for scientific experiments, but also how well you apply them in the lab. After all, what use is it being able to remember something you don't understand and are not able to use?

This is where the GCSE scores – it is designed to test ALL your skills.

2. GCSE AND THE NATIONAL CURRICULUM

What is the National Curriculum?

The Education Reform Act of 1988 requires all schools in the maintained sector to provide a broad and balanced curriculum for students of compulsory school age. This is known as the National Curriculum.

What subjects are included in the National Curriculum?

Basically, the National Curriculum consists of eleven subjects – with Welsh as an additional subject for Welsh-speaking schools.

In Key Stages (KS) 1–3, the following subjects are included in the National Curriculum:

- English
- Mathematics
- Science
- Design & Technology
- Information Technology
- History
- Geography
- Art
- Music
- Physical Education
- and a Modern Foreign Language (in KS3)

At KS4, the range of subjects that students may study and in which they may be tested is increased, but the only subjects for which programmes of study remain compulsory are:

- English
- Mathematics
- Science
- Design & Technology*

- Modern Foreign Language*
- Information Technology*
- Physical Education

** not a statutory requirement in Wales*

In Wales, Welsh is added for schools that are not Welsh-speaking. Wales also has separate subject Orders from England in History, Geography, Art, Music and Welsh.

Schools in England and Wales also have a statutory duty to provide identified Religious Education and Sex Education. With Sex Education, as with Religious Education, parents can choose not to let their child study the subject, except for the elements of Sex Education required by the National Curriculum (ie human growth and reproduction).

In the future (probably from 1998) Careers Education will also have to be part of the school curriculum in both England and Wales, but with no statutory examination requirement.

What effect does the National Curriculum have on GCSE?

There are National Curriculum guidelines on the knowledge, skills and understanding that all pupils are expected to have acquired in each subject by the ages of 7 (age 8 in Northern Ireland), 11, 14 and 16.

GCSE is at present the main means of assessing what students have achieved in each subject during KS4. GNVQ is also likely to make a significant contribution for an increasing number of young people – either through the experience of specific units or through the Part One GNVQ qualification. There is further information on the role of GNVQ in KS4 in Chapter 7.

GCSE criteria have gone through a lengthy revision process, in line with the National Curriculum itself. The revised National Curriculum Orders (1995) resulted in further revisions in GCSE criteria and the examining groups have prepared new syllabuses. These new syllabuses take account of the latest thinking on what knowledge, understanding and skills young people ought to be acquiring through their studies.

Progression and continuity are also receiving greater emphasis, with the need, for example, to ensure the appropriate links between KS3 and KS4.

The following new GCSE syllabuses are available for National Curriculum and related subjects for examination in 1998:

- Art (short and full courses)
- Design & Technology (short and full courses)
- English
- English Literature
- Geography (short and full courses)
- History (short and full courses)
- Home Economics
- Information Systems
- Information Technology (short and full courses)
- Mathematics
- Modern Foreign Languages (short and full courses)
- Music (short and full courses)
- Physical Education (short and full courses)
- Science (single and double award)
- Science: Biology
- Science: Chemistry
- Science: Physics
- Welsh
- Welsh Literature
- Welsh Second Language (short and full courses)

Some other subjects governed by subject-specific GCSE criteria already have new syllabuses. The first examinations in these subjects were held in Summer 1996:

- Business Studies
- Classical Civilisation
- Economics
- Greek
- Latin
- Law
- Politics
- Psychology
- Religious Studies

- Science: Environmental
- Science: Geology
- Science: Rural
- Social Science
- Sociology

All remaining GCSE subjects will have new syllabuses available for examination in 1999, ie with courses starting in September 1997. In the case of National Curriculum subjects, all the new syllabuses cover the KS4 programmes of study. These programmes of study define the essential content of each subject and are the basis for planning, teaching, learning and assessment objectives.

There are also a number of approved syllabuses in subjects which do not have subject-specific criteria. These syllabuses are governed by GCSE Regulations, as distinct from the National Curriculum Orders. The first syllabuses of this nature to be approved were:

- Accounting
- Administration
- Agriculture & Horticulture
- Archaeology
- Astronomy
- British Industrial Society
- Catering
- Communication Studies
- Critical Studies in Art
- Drama & Theatre Arts
- Electronics
- Environmental Studies
- General Studies
- Health Studies
- Information Studies
- Media Studies
- Nautical Studies
- Office Applications
- Performing Arts: Dance
- Statistics
- Travel & Tourism

Will this make a difference to me? Will I have no choice about taking National Curriculum subjects?

The National Curriculum takes some of the optional element out of the 14–16 stage. Most students will take GCSEs in English, Mathematics and Science. For Science, you may take:

- a Double Award exam (equal to two GCSEs) that covers Biology, Chemistry and Physics
- separate exams in these three science subjects, or
- a Single Award exam (one GCSE) that covers all three science subjects, but less fully than the Double Award

The Science option that you are offered may depend to some extent on your school's curriculum policies. But the government believes that Double Science or the three separate sciences should be taken by the great majority of students. The alternative Single Science course is intended for a minority of students who may need, for whatever reason, to spend more time on other subjects.

Single Science is designed to be just as challenging at all levels, and will lead to a single award GCSE. One important point is that the student who takes Single Science but who then wishes to take A-level Science post-16 may need a bridging course before (or at the start of) the A-levels.

In Design & Technology a revised Technology Order was introduced for KS4 in 1996 and Design & Technology is now compulsory for all students entering KS4.

The National Curriculum is not intended to be a straitjacket and the review of the National Curriculum carried out by Sir Ron Dearing has led to greater flexibility. At KS4, it is intended that the statutory curriculum should occupy about 60% of the time, leaving 40% available for other options.

In Wales, there is even more time for schools to use as they choose – half the timetable as opposed to 40% in England – because there are no requirements for Modern Foreign Languages, Technology or Information Technology.

What will this flexibility mean for me?

Firstly, there is more choice of courses in some subjects. These courses will require different amounts of time on the timetable and will lead to different qualifications.

Short courses, as an alternative to a full GCSE, are available in subjects like Art, Design & Technology, Geography, History, Information Technology, Modern Foreign Languages, Music, Physical Education, Religious Education and Welsh Second Language. Such courses have half the value of a full GCSE and take up half the teaching time – so they might, for example, be completed in one year rather than the usual two. Short courses are graded on the same scale as the full GCSE, but cover fewer topics. They count as half a GCSE.

You can use the short courses in different ways.

- More able students can use them as a way of taking more subjects, eg fitting in a second foreign language that might not otherwise be possible.
- If other subject choices prevent you from taking a full GCSE, you can still gain a short-course qualification in a subject like Art, Geography, Information Technology, Physical Education or Religious Education.
- If you think that you may need extra time to study a particular subject, taking a short course GCSE in the time taken by a full GCSE course may be an attractive proposition.

Remember that you will be allowed to drop one or more subjects at the end of KS3, if this seems a good option for you.

Also, you will be able, either individually or on a whole class basis, to take GCSE early and then to drop the subjects that have been taken.

Finally, the vocational examining bodies, such as City & Guilds, Edexcel and RSA, provide an alternative to GCSE. More information about alternatives to GCSE is given at the end of this chapter.

What will be the effects of my taking one or more GCSEs early?

There are specific National Curriculum Regulations which apply to whole classes of students taking GCSE (or equivalent) qualifications early. Under these Regulations, students who take GCSE (or an equivalent qualification) in a National Curriculum subject at the same time as the majority of students in their class, and before the start of the second year of KS4 will thereafter be excepted from the National Curriculum requirements relating to that subject. This exception applies irrespective of the level attained by the student in the examination. However, it does not apply to a short course, when both a full course and a short course are specified for the particular National Curriculum subject.

What are the alternatives to GCSE?

The General National Vocational Qualification (GNVQ) has already become a popular alternative to A-level or GCSE study post-16 in school sixth forms and in colleges.

GNVQ courses are offered at Foundation, Intermediate and Advanced levels and provide you with work-related knowledge, skills and understanding. Students are expected to acquire the basic skills and a body of knowledge relevant to a particular vocational area, such as Art & Design, Business, Health & Social Care, Leisure & Tourism, or Manufacturing.

For more general information about GNVQs at Key Stage 4, see Chapter 7 – The GNVQ Alternative. Additional information about GNVQs post-16 is contained in Chapter 13 – Life After GCSE.

Is there anything else beside GCSE and GNVQ?

Yes, there are a few other qualifications that your school might be offering at KS4, below the level of GCSE or GNVQ. Such qualifications have to feature on an approved list published by the Department for Education and Employment (DfEE) and the Qualifications and Curriculum Authority (QCA). They include:

- certain qualifications in Literacy, Numeracy and Information

Technology which are meant to offer progression towards GCSE or the NCVQ key skills units
- some qualifications in other National Curriculum subjects

Some students will not be entered for GCSE in a National Curriculum subject nor for a designated qualification relating to that subject below GCSE. For such students, teacher assessment of performance at the end of KS4 will be recorded, normally via the National Record of Achievement.

Essentially, the range of possible courses at KS4 is as follows:

- full GCSEs
- GCSE short courses
- Part One GNVQs
- full GNVQs in approved subjects
- individual units from approved GNVQ subjects
- GNVQ language units
- the Information Technology key skills unit
- NVQs or NVQ units
- qualifications below GCSE or GNVQ (see Chapter 10).

Where Welsh is a core subject, students will take Welsh to GCSE. In schools where Welsh is a non-core foundation subject, students will study Welsh at KS4, but not necessarily to GCSE. A short course is available in Welsh as a second language. GNVQ Welsh Language units are also being piloted for KS4 students studying Welsh as a second language and are expected to be more generally available from September 1999.

3. HOW THE GCSE EXAM WORKS

There are eight different examining groups that set examinations for GCSE and GNVQs at KS4:

The Midland Examining Group (MEG)
The Northern Examinations and Assessment Board (NEAB)
The Southern Examining Group (SEG)
The Welsh Joint Education Committee (WJEC)
The Edexcel Foundation (Edexcel)
City & Guilds of London Institute (City & Guilds)
RSA Examinations Board (RSA)
The Northern Ireland Council for the Curriculum, Examinations and Assessment (CCEA)

Your school will normally be free to select courses of study set by any of the examining groups. Most teachers look carefully at the full range of syllabuses to find the course that seems the most interesting and useful – the one they hope you will enjoy and do best in.

With different groups setting the exams in the same subjects, do standards vary?

In the past, government statements and reports from HMI have raised some concern about the consistency of standards. In particular, the examining groups are being encouraged to apply more objective criteria for awarding and to be more rigorous in approaches and procedures across the groups.

GCSE general criteria from QCA provide overall guidance on subject titles, the nature of syllabuses, assessment procedures and the general conduct of examinations. These general criteria require each syllabus to promote a balance of knowledge, understanding and skills. They also demand that student achievement in each syllabus is assessed through a combination of coursework and terminal examination appropriate to the subject.

In England, Wales and Northern Ireland the examining groups

together form the Joint Council for the GCSE. The Joint Council provides a forum for discussion and the exchange of information. It is responsible for coordinating the work of the individual groups and helping to establish nationally consistent practices. The examining groups, for example, collaborated over the preparation of GCSE syllabuses for the National Curriculum core subjects of English, Mathematics and Science. Each group puts forward proposals to the Joint Council. From these proposals a range of syllabuses was agreed by the Joint Council for the GCSE. As a consequence, for each core subject there are now syllabuses catering for the full range of needs.

All these moves should ensure that syllabuses have the highest possible degree of consistency. QCA works closely with the Joint Council and the individual examining groups to maintain GCSE standards and to continue to improve the effectiveness and fairness of the system.

Further action to ensure that standards are being maintained in both GCSE and A-level examinations was initiated by the previous government, following the publication of a SCAA/OFSTED report on examinations. 'Standards in Public Examinations 1975 to 1995' analysed evidence relating to examination standards and candidates' performance in English, Mathematics and Chemistry at both GCSE and A-level over a period of 20 years.

The report's main conclusion was that the performance required for a given grade has remained broadly the same. However, two additional findings help to explain the common public view that examinations are somehow 'softer' than they used to be:

- there has been a broadening of content in most of the subjects, which means that candidates have to be familiar with more material; and

- as a result, there has been a reduced emphasis on some topics within subjects, such as reasoning and extended problem solving in Mathematics.

Copies of this report are available from QCA Publications on 0181 867 3299 or via fax on 0181 813 6564 (priced £3).

How is the GCSE graded?

The grading system is based on an A–G scale. In addition, a 'starred' A grade (A*) has been available since 1994.

Examiners decide the grade boundaries for the award of grades A, C and F. The remaining grades are then awarded on an arithmetical basis. For example, for a particular syllabus the grade A boundary might be set at 300 marks and the grade C boundary at 220 marks. The grade B boundary would then be set halfway, at 260 marks.

In Modern Foreign Languages, there is a separate awarding system. A range of points – usually 7 – is available for each of the four language skills. GCSE grades are awarded on the number of points achieved in the subject as a whole. So, for example, an A grade is awarded for candidates who achieve 24 or more of the 28 points usually available.

In order to help parents understand the level of attainment signified by the GCSE grade awarded, 'attainment descriptions' are offered that relate to grades A, C and F and below G.

How difficult is it to achieve the A*?

There is no limit on the number of starred A grades awarded in any one subject. Results depend on the quality of the candidates' work and on where the awarding body draws its other grade boundaries.

What happens if my GCSE performance does not earn a grade G or above?

If that does happen, the performance is reported on the results slip as U (for 'unclassified').

How will the marks for my GCSE be arrived at?

In most subjects, the marks are made up of two parts. Firstly, coursework done in Years 10 and 11 (Years 11 and 12 in Northern Ireland) is assessed. Secondly, an examination is held at the end of the two years. This is explained more fully in the next chapter.

Will I lose marks for bad spelling?

QCA has developed marking criteria for use in GCSE terminal examinations. They apply to all subjects where candidates are required to write in sentences (in English or Welsh). They apply to all GCSE written papers and written coursework, but not to multiple choice or practical tests.

For each GCSE subject, 5% of the marks for each written paper are allocated to spelling, punctuation and grammar according to the following performance criteria:

- *Threshold performance:* candidates spell, punctuate and use the rules of grammar with reasonable accuracy; they use a limited range of specialist terms appropriately.

- *Intermediate performance:* candidates spell, punctuate and use the rules of grammar with considerable accuracy; they use a good range of specialist terms with facility.

- *High performance:* candidates spell, punctuate and use the rules of grammar with almost faultless accuracy, using a range of grammatical constructions; they also use a wide range of specialist terms adeptly and with precision.

Candidates below the threshold performance level receive no marks for spelling, punctuation and grammar.

Although these criteria apply equally to all subjects, the overall effect on the whole subject grade is clearly greater in those subjects where there is a larger writing component.

The assessment criteria for English and Welsh make additional requirements for linguistic accuracy. Performance in spelling, punctuation and grammar is a factor in determining the candidate's overall grade.

Marks are allocated for spelling in GCSE written coursework on the same basis as for GCSE terminal examinations.

There are special arrangements to exempt dyslexic and other students with disabilities from this requirement.

Does this mean that dictionaries cannot be used in examinations?

Dictionaries and spelling aids are no longer allowed, except for certain vocationally slanted examinations and for candidates who are permitted to use a bilingual dictionary (after the school has made a special representation to which the examining group has agreed).

Do employers understand what GCSEs are?

Every attempt has been made to acquaint employers with recent changes. But you might still find yourself faced with a bewildered employer or personnel officer. Don't worry… help is available. On the back of the examination certificate you will receive, there is an explanation of how the exam works.

4. COURSEWORK IN FOCUS

We've mentioned 'coursework' several times. Now it's time to look at it in more detail.

What is coursework?

Coursework is work which is integral to the course. That means that it is usually done in class and is closely supervised by teachers.

It can take various forms such as assignments in English and History; fieldwork in Geography; practical and project work in Art, Mathematics, Technology and Science; compositions in Music.

Throughout your two years of study for GCSEs your teacher will set specific topics for you. These topics will be marked by your teacher and those marks will go towards your final GCSE results.

Why is coursework necessary?

As mentioned previously, many skills can't be tested by the traditional written exam – practical and oral skills, for example. Coursework gives you the chance to demonstrate the many abilities you have and so makes the final mark you receive much fairer.

Teachers, with support from the examining groups, are responsible for ensuring that students are engaged in suitable coursework, which is normally an essential ingredient to meet the specific subject requirements of the National Curriculum. Recent HMI and OFSTED reports on quality and standards in GCSE examinations have found that both teacher assessment and the guidance provided by the examining groups to support teacher assessment of coursework are generally of a high standard.

Which skills are tested through coursework?

Your performance in coursework will show if you are able:

- to research, collect, compare and organise information

- to work in a group
- to make accurate records and use your powers of observation through laboratory and field work
- to plan and organise a long piece of work
- to use apparatus and machinery
- to communicate – and that means to listen as well as to talk and discuss
- to investigate, plan and design.

These are exactly the vocationally related skills employers value.

Coursework also encourages young people to work independently and helps them prepare for higher level studies, such as A-levels and AS-levels and GNVQ Advanced courses.

When will I do the coursework?

In some subjects you will start coursework during the first term of Year 10 (Year 11 in Northern Ireland), while with other subjects coursework may not start until Year 11 (Year 12 in Northern Ireland). It will all depend on the syllabus.

Yes, but *when* will I actually do coursework? Will it cut into my spare time?

Some of the work will be done in class, some will be done as homework. Though your teachers may say it shouldn't take you any longer than your normal homework, it's only fair to say that if you want to do well, it probably will take more time.

Is there coursework in all subjects?

Most Modern Foreign Languages include an oral, but there isn't necessarily any other coursework.

What percentage of marks is given for coursework?

There must always be an externally set terminal examination. In the case of modular syllabuses, the terminal examination must account for at least 50% of the marks. The weighting for coursework in all other syllabuses is set out below:

Art	up to 60%
Design & Technology	at least 40% and up to 60%
English	up to 40%
English Literature	up to 30%
Geography	at least 20% and up to 25%
History	up to 25%
Home Economics	up to 50%
Information Technology	at least 40% and up to 60%
Mathematics	up to 20%
Modern Foreign Languages	up to 30%
Music	up to 60%
Physical Education	at least 60% and up to 70%
Science	at least 25% and up to 30%
Welsh	at least 30% and up to 40%
Welsh Literature	up to 30%
Welsh Second Language	up to 40%

It sounds as though I am going to have to take a lot of exams

It depends on how you look at it.

Your ability will be tested throughout the two years. But your coursework performance will in some cases enable you to go into the examination well on your way to a good grade.

What if six different teachers give me coursework at the same time – I'll be a wreck!

Coursework overload is a possible hazard of the GCSE. Your teachers will be anxious to avoid overloading you. Nobody can tackle a great number of big assignments at the same time and do them all well – and your teachers do want you to do well.

In a well-run school, coursework overload should not happen. Before the two-year course begins, teachers usually get together and work out a timetable for setting coursework assignments. But even the best run systems can break down. So, be alert... if you are given too much coursework at any one time, don't keep your worries to yourself. Tell your teachers about the problem immediately.

No doubt you will find yourself working harder than you have had to before, but, remember, your teachers are not trying to work you to a standstill. It is in their interests as well as yours that you should do well.

Coursework is to your advantage

GCSE has been widely praised for allowing candidates to demonstrate what they know, understand and can do.

Coursework allows a wider range of skills to be assessed than is possible in a written examination. Evidence suggests that coursework assessment increases candidates' motivation.

- If you are a good communicator you'll have the chance to prove it
- If you are a painstaking perfectionist you'll have the time to perfect your work and so earn marks for it
- If you are a thinker you'll have time to think
- If you are a problem solver you'll get the time to find the solution

But... it's no good leaving everything to the last minute with GCSE. You won't get through by copying someone else's notes the day before the exam. You'll need to work throughout the two years to do well – and work hard. Sorry, but there's no escape.

What if I'm ill when an assessment is due?

You'll find that the deadlines set for coursework are quite flexible, so the odd week, even a month of illness, should not set you back too much.

But what if I'm away for a term or longer?

Most teachers and examining groups are very sympathetic if you are ill and will try to find a way for you to complete the course.

There are no hard and fast rules... subjects vary, and so do individual cases. But if you have completed enough pieces of coursework over the two years, they can usually assess how well you are likely to do, and give you a fair mark.

However, one thing is certain: both your school and examining group want you to take the exam and will do their best to help you. So, if you know you are going to miss school for some reason, tell your teachers as soon as possible, so that they can make alternative arrangements for you.

What happens if I change schools in the middle of my GCSE?

It should not be too difficult for you to change from a course set by one examining group to one set by another because they will both be assessing the same skills.

In addition, you might be able to transfer any coursework you have already completed. But – and it is a very big BUT – it depends on what subjects you are taking. The Joint Council for the GCSE certainly recommends that assessment across syllabuses from more than one examining group should be allowed.

For example, it is much easier to move from one syllabus to another in Maths or a Modern Foreign Language than it is, say in History, where you could be studying a different historical period. And in English Literature the set books are unlikely to be the same, so, again, transfer tends to be more difficult.

If you are well advanced in your original studies when you make the move, arrangements can be made for you to take the exam in your original course in your new school. Your teachers and the examiners will try and do their best for each student, so your case would be treated sympathetically.

My teacher doesn't like me. Will it affect my assessment marks?

No.

Equally, you can't be upgraded by your teacher either. You can rest assured there will be neither discrimination nor favouritism in your GCSE assessment. No teacher would allow any personal feelings to influence the results of a public examination. Besides which, there are too many checks and safeguards… so, it couldn't happen anyway. And all research shows that coursework is no less reliable than written examinations.

What's to stop someone else doing my coursework for me?

The work which you submit for assessment must be your own. Teachers have to certify that coursework has been supervised properly. And teachers are usually very shrewd: they know what most of their students are capable of.

If you quote from any books or other materials, you should state which sources you have used. And, if you receive guidance from someone other than your teacher, you should tell your teacher, who will then record the nature of the assistance.

Some teachers expect more of their students than others and so mark stiffly – how can the courses be completely fair?

Teachers are provided with resource packs for use in preparing coursework, together with examples of candidates' work from previous examinations to demonstrate the standards required. There are also opportunities to talk with other teachers and moderators from the examining groups at meetings, in order to standardise work from the current examination.

What is a moderator?

The moderator is somebody outside your school who will look at the work of your class in relation to the coursework done by other schools. If the moderator thinks your teacher has marked too harshly or too leniently, compared with other teachers, then the marks will be adjusted to bring them into line.

So the system is doubly fair because more than one person will be marking your work.

Will I know what marks I get for my coursework?

Your school might tell you how well you have done in individual pieces of work, but you are unlikely to be told your overall coursework mark – after all, the moderator system may see it changed.

5. THE EXAM UNDER EXAMINATION

After you've put in all the hard work over two years, what about the last hurdle – the exam itself?

Probably the greatest difference between school examinations and the GCSE examinations is time. In most schools, the end-of-year exams are concentrated into approximately two weeks, maybe less. This is possible because most schools do not offer a very large number of subjects. So the exams come thick and fast, often two or three in a day.

It's very different with the GCSE. Exams are spread over a much longer period of time – so you should find that your exams are well spaced out with free days in between. Great – more time for revision! But then you may need more time because you'll be tested on two years' work. The timetable for exams is drawn up well in advance, so you should know the term before the exams start when you will actually sit each paper.

When I come to take my exams, will subjects clash on the timetable?

Each year the six examining groups get together and draw up a common timetable to avoid possible clashes of exams for students taking subjects from different groups.

Will we really all do the same exam papers?

No. In most subjects, alternative papers exist and teachers, supported by examining groups, are responsible for ensuring that students are entered for papers which set appropriate targets. This is in addition to the different types and levels of work that students undertake in coursework, which is also chosen in consultation with teachers.

In most cases, students will actually sit different papers according to their own abilities. This process is known as 'tiering' and from 1998 most large-entry GCSE subjects are to be examined through a foundation tier covering grades C to G and a higher, overlapping tier covering grades A* to D.

For each tier of entry, the written question papers will:

- be at an appropriate level of difficulty for the range of grades available at that tier
- encourage the more able to respond at a greater depth
- provide opportunities for the less able to show what they know
- use appropriate language.

In Maths, there are three overlapping tiers and separate content is defined in the syllabuses for each tier of entry. From 1998, the highest tier will include material targeted at candidates expected to achieve grades A*–B, but grade C is still available for students who perform less well than expected. The intermediate tier will include more material targeted at candidates expected to achieve grades B and C.

In Art, History, Humanities, Music, Performing Arts, Physical Education and Religious Studies questions can be set which allow all students to respond effectively at their own level. Examination papers are therefore designed to cover the full grade range, without the need for tiering.

Will short courses be tiered?

Yes. The tiering arrangements for GCSE short courses match those for the full GCSEs in the same subject.

In Combined Subject GCSEs, the tiering arrangements for each subject will be the same as those for the full GCSE in that subject. For example, in GCSE Art and IT (Combined Subject) there will be no tiered papers in the Art component but the IT component will have tiered written papers.

Coursework is another way of enabling candidates to demonstrate differentiated ability, with the additional advantages of an unpressured environment and access to guidance from a teacher.

It all sounds a bit complicated to me!

If it sounds a complicated system, don't worry. Before you get anywhere near taking the exams, your teacher will tell you which kind of paper you will be taking in each subject. They will also probably show you examples of what the exam papers will look like and you'll have a chance to try them out. Don't worry, you will be in no doubt about what to do, and what's expected of you when you take the exam.

I just can't do exams, I go to pieces. Is there any hope for me?

The good news is that the GCSE does help people like you. If you choose the subjects that best suit you, work consistently and well at your coursework and then revise thoroughly for the final examination, you should do well.

Will the GCSE give me a fair deal?

Most people think so and here are the reasons why:

- it is fair because it tests all your skills
- the courses are interesting and relevant
- everybody has the same chance of success because you all take the same exam and succeed at your own level.

6. CHOOSING THE RIGHT SUBJECTS

Subjects that can be taken at GCSE (as full courses)

Accounting
Agricultural Science
American Studies
Applied Science
Arabic
Arabic, Chinese & Japanese
Archaeology
Art
Art (Modular)
Art & Design
Astronomy

Bengali
Biblical Hebrew
Biology
Biology (Human)
British Government & Politics
British Industrial Society
Building Studies
Business Studies
Business Studies & Economics
Business & Information Studies

Catering
CDT (Craft, Design & Technology): Design & Communication
CDT: Design & Realisation
CDT: Technology
Chemistry
Chinese
Classical Civilisation
Classical Subjects: Greek
Classical Subjects: Latin
Commerce
Communication Studies
Community Issues
Computer Studies
Control Technology
Creative Arts
Critical Studies in Art & Design

Dance
Design
Design & Communication
Design & Realisation
Design & Technology
Design & Technology and Automation
Design & Technology and Built Environment
Design & Technology and Business Studies
Design & Technology and Catering
Design & Technology and Child Development
Design & Technology and Electronics
Design & Technology and Fashion
Design & Technology: Electronic Products
Design & Technology: Food Technology

Design & Technology: Graphic Products
Design & Technology: Resistant Materials Technology
Design & Technology: Textile Technology
Design Centred Studies
Drama
Drama & Expressive Arts
Drama & Theatre Arts
Drama: Community Theatre

Economics
Electronics
Engineering Workshop Theory & Practice
English
English Literature
Environmental Science
Environmental Studies
European Arts
European Studies
Expressive Arts

French
French & Business Studies

General Studies
Geography
Geography & Business Studies
Geography & History
Geology
German
German & Business Studies
Graphic & Technical Communication
Graphical Communication
Greek
Greek Civilisation
Gujarati

Health Studies
Hindi
History
History (Britain, Europe & the World 19th/20th C)
History (British 19th & 20th C)
History (British & European)
History (Economic & Social)
History (British, Social & Economic)
History (English History 16th & 17th C)
History (Modern World/ 20th C)
History (Schools History Project)
History (Social and Industrial History of England & Wales, 18th & 19th C)
History of Art & Design
Home Economics
Home Economics: Child Development
Home Economics: Family, Home & Food
Home Economics: Food
Home Economics: Food & Nutrition
Home Economics: Home & Family
Home Economics: Textiles
Humanities

Information Studies
Information Systems
Information Systems (Business)

Information Technology
Information Technology & Business Studies
Integrated Humanities
Italian

Japanese

Keyboard Applications

Land Surveying
Latin
Latin & Roman Civilisation
Law
Law in Society

Marine Navigation
Mathematics
Mathematics (SMP)
Mathematical Studies
Media Studies
Modern European Languages
Modern Foreign Languages & Business Studies
Modern Greek
Modern Greek & Turkish
Modern Hebrew
Motor Vehicle Studies
Music

Nautical Studies
Navigation

Office Applications
Office Skills
Office Studies
Office Technology

Panjabi
Persian
Photography
Physical Education
Physical Education (Games)
Physics
Polish
Political Studies
Politics & Government
Portuguese
Psychology
Psychology (Child Development)

Religious Education
Religious Studies
Religious Studies (Islam)
Resistant Materials Technology & Business Studies
Rural Science
Russian
Russian Studies

Science
Science (Biology, Chemistry & Physics)
Science (Geology, Rural & Environmental)
Science: Double Award (Combined)
Science: Single Award (Combined)
Science: Double & Single Award (Combined)
Science: Human Physiology & Health
Science, Technology & Society
Social Science
Sociology
Spanish

Spanish & Business Studies
Statistics
Surveying

Technical Communication
Technology
Technology & Business Studies
Technology & Electronics
Technology & Organisations
Textiles
Travel & Tourism

Turkish

Ukrainian
Understanding Industrial Society
Urdu

Welfare & Society
Welsh
Welsh Literature
Welsh Second Language
World Development

How to choose the right subjects

Because young people frequently change their career ideas at this stage, most schools have always put some restrictions on choice of subject. The National Curriculum ensures that you keep your options open by not specialising too narrowly at an early stage.

The National Curriculum limits the number of choices that have to be made by young people during Year 9 (Year 10 in Northern Ireland), but when there are still choices to be made, how should you set about choosing?

1. *Ask yourself:* What do I want to do when I leave school?

(a) If you know exactly what career you want to follow then turn to Chapter 9 and see what GCSE subjects are required.

(b) If you are thinking of studying for a degree eventually, then take a look at a couple of publications that are likely to be available in your school or college careers library – *University and College Entrance: The Official Guide*, published by the Universities and Colleges Admissions Service (UCAS) and *The Complete Degree Course Offers for Entry into Higher Education* by Brian Heap (also available on CD-ROM). These excellent guides give all the essential information about the choice of higher education, including details of the subjects required for different higher education courses.

(c) If you've no idea, don't worry. You are probably in the majority... 13 or 14 is an early age to decide on a career. Your aim now should be to choose a selection of subjects that will keep as many career doors open as possible.

2. *Ask yourself:*
What am I good at and what do I enjoy doing?

Are any of the available GCSE subjects closely related to these interests? Now add any subjects you think are essential to your chosen career. Already you are beginning to get a list.

3. *Ask yourself:*
Which subjects are most likely to be on offer at my school?

Here is a list of the subjects most likely to be offered by schools.

MATHS

ENGLISH
Language
Literature

SCIENCES
Biology
Chemistry
Physics
Science
Single or Double Award

TECHNOLOGY
Business Studies
Design & Technology
Information Technology

HUMANITIES
Geography
History
Religious Education

EXPRESSIVE ARTS
Art
Dance
Drama
Music

MODERN LANGUAGES
French
German
Spanish

4. *Ask yourself:*
What about other options?

Before you make your final choice, remember – the GCSE offers a range of subjects you've probably never tried before. Many schools will organise a few sample lessons in the 'new' subjects they offer , to give you some idea of what they are like. These subjects could be useful, even a deciding factor to your future career, so give them serious consideration.

You may well now have a list as long as your arm, so the next question must be...

5. *Ask yourself:*
How many subjects should I take?

As many as you are capable of doing well. Most students would say that it is better to get a C or D grade in six subjects, rather than a G in nine. It is well worth listening to the advice of your teachers about getting the balance right.

Coursework overload

Don't overburden yourself with coursework.

Some subjects involve more research-based coursework to be done outside the classroom. History and Geography are examples of this. Maths and Modern Foreign Languages, on the other hand, will probably include very little. As it is important that you have sufficient time to do every project well, make sure you get the workload right by not picking too many subjects that are heavy on coursework. So, check coursework content with your teachers.

What are modular courses?

Modular schemes offer students the opportunity to study relatively small parts of the curriculum in a concentrated period. Each unit or module contains very specific and understandable learning targets, with the student's learning assessed at the end of each module.

The different structure of modular courses, with a heavy emphasis on assessment and systematic feedback between teacher and student, suits some students better than the more traditional structure.

In most subjects except Design & Technology, at least 60% of the marks will still come from terminal examinations. In addition, end-of-unit tests which count towards the final assessment will be externally set and marked; and any marks allocated for coursework will be set at the same limit as for the ordinary GCSE in that subject.

And finally

Your teachers will see it as part of their responsibility to ensure you are entered for the most appropriate subjects and syllabuses available. So, before opting for, or committing yourself to, any course, make sure that you ask each subject teacher:

- how much reading is involved
- how much writing is involved
- how much coursework is involved;
- what percentage of the marks is given for coursework
- if there's the option of different tiers of assessment
- if there's an oral test
- if you'll have to gather information for yourself
- if projects are involved
- what practical skills are involved
- how much laboratory or fieldwork is involved.

With this information, you should be well placed to begin to make your GCSE decisions.

7. THE GNVQ ALTERNATIVE

What is GNVQ?

GNVQ stands for General National Vocational Qualification. GNVQ courses are intended to provide you with the knowledge, skills and understanding you need for work in a broad vocational area. Students are expected to acquire the basic skills and a body of knowledge relevant to a particular vocational area. GNVQs do not provide training for a specific job.

The courses are offered at Foundation, Intermediate and Advanced levels (although the Advanced level is not available at Key Stage 4).

In addition to acquiring the basic skills and a body of knowledge relevant to one of the vocational areas, all students have to achieve a range of key skills (previously known as 'core skills'). Evidence of achievement, at an appropriate level, is required in three key skill units: Communication, Application of Number and Information Technology.

But how does GNVQ fit in at Key Stage 4?

The GNVQ is now becoming the basis for alternative vocational pathways at KS4. The aim is to assist progression into a vocational route post-16 and provide a foundation for further education and/or training within the National Vocational Qualification (NVQ) framework.

There are several ways in which you may have some involvement with GNVQs at KS4. These will all complement the National Curriculum – and remember that all students must take the GCSE or equivalent in Maths, English and Science – and can help provide a more appropriate route. About 14% of all secondary schools in England (and a considerably higher percentage in Wales) have been involved in a national Part One GNVQ pilot aimed at developing a new curriculum framework for 14–16 students.

What is Part One GNVQ?

It is a new curriculum framework that enables students to combine GCSE (or a vocational qualification equivalent to GCSE) in the compulsory subjects with other National Curriculum subjects and other subjects or courses which lead to vocational qualifications.

Part One itself has been designed to take 20% of the curriculum time in KS4. It offers a package of GNVQ units (or modules). Part One is available at two levels:

- at Foundation level – broadly equivalent to two GCSEs at grades D–G
- at Intermediate level – broadly equivalent to two GCSEs at grades A*–C.

Part One results will feature in school performance tables and it is intended that the Part One structure should be available to all schools from September 1998.

What subjects are available at Part One?

Seven vocational areas are currently offered:

- Art & Design
- Business
- Engineering
- Health & Social Care
- Information Technology
- Leisure & Tourism
- Manufacturing

The chosen vocational area is taken over the two-year period of KS4. The course is made up of self-contained units (or modules), including three vocational units and three units in the mandatory key skills of Communication, Application of Number and Information Technology. To take the example of a Part One in Business at Intermediate level, the three vocational units are:

- Business organisations and employment

- Students in business organisations
- Consumers and customers

Can you tell me a bit more about the key skills?

As mentioned above, all GNVQ candidates have to achieve key skills in Communication, Application of Number and Information Technology. The intention is to encourage a more integrated approach to the teaching of such skills across subject boundaries. For example, revision of the National Curriculum Subject Orders has taken account of GNVQ key skill requirements. So GCSE English contributes to key skill Communication and GCSE Maths to key skill Application of Number. The National Curriculum programme of study for Information Technology (whether taken as a GCSE course or not) makes a similar contribution to the key skill Information Technology.

There are two further key skills which are not formally accredited in the final award, but in which all GNVQ candidates have had regular practice: Improving own Learning and Performance (or 'Learning how to learn') and Working with Others. Like the mandatory key skills, these are acquired in a work-related context and this is one aspect of GNVQs that makes them attractive to employers.

Remember that students taking Part One at KS4 must still follow the National Curriculum in English, Mathematics, Science, Physical Education, Technology and a Modern Foreign Language. They will also follow complementary programmes which include Religious Education, Sex Education and Careers Education.

How are GNVQs assessed?

In GNVQs, you are assessed on the work you do during the course. All assessments are carried out by qualified assessors, mostly by school staff who have qualified as assessors. Each GNVQ is made up of a specified number of mandatory and optional units. You will have to do a short multiple-choice test for each mandatory unit.

The assessment for Part One GNVQ courses consists of four elements:

- a portfolio containing students' work in the three vocational units, assessed by teachers and checked both within the school and by the vocational awarding body (City & Guilds, Edexcel or RSA)
- evidence of attainment in the key skills, with teachers' assessments checked both within the school and by the vocational awarding body
- end-of-unit tests, set and marked by the awarding body, checking the coverage of the knowledge requirements of each vocational unit
- extension tests checking depth of understanding for students aiming at the high grades of Merit or Distinction.

Can I be sure that GNVQs are as high a standard as GCSEs?

GNVQs meet strict standards approved by the QCA, the merged body formed from the SCAA and the NCVQ, set up by the government. An OFSTED report on the early progress of the Part One GNVQ pilot found that the courses helped motivate students and demanded a high degree of commitment from both students and teachers. Part One teaching and learning opportunities were found to encourage young people:

- to assume responsibility for their own learning
- to meet deadlines
- to manage their time effectively
- to take the initiative in organising their work.

Parents and teachers commented favourably on the way students were motivated and showed commitment to their work.

Where does Part One lead?

The Part One qualification offers several different progression routes:

- adding the three further units needed to complete the full GNVQ at the same level

- moving up to the next level, ie from Foundation to Intermediate or from Intermediate to Advanced
- taking A-level and/or AS-level courses
- following a mixed programme, eg combining GCSEs or A-levels (or Advanced GNVQ) with a vocational or occupational course
- going into employment
- going on to further, more occupationally specific training, eg working towards NVQs (usually from the base of a job or traineeship).

How else can I be involved in GNVQs at Key Stage 4?

The other options which involve GNVQ or NVQ include:

- *Taking a full Intermediate or Foundation GNVQ at KS4.* This would mean that there would be no time for subjects outside the mandatory curriculum, as it would take up 30–40% of curriculum time. This is not an attractive alternative for many schools, although one barrier to acceptability has now been removed, with the DfEE agreeing that any full GNVQs taken pre-16 (as with Part One GNVQ) will be recognised in the performance tables published annually by the government.

- *GNVQ Vocational Units.* In some schools, students will be able to take specific vocational units of interest. Unit credits gained in this way can count towards a full GNVQ taken at a later stage. However, at present unit certification does not feature in school performance tables.

- *NCVQ Units in Information Technology.* It is possible to take a freestanding unit in IT, although this does not cover the full National Curriculum requirement for Key Stage 4. The unit needs to be taken within the context of a broader course, eg within a vocational unit of GNVQ IT.

- *GNVQ Language Units.* These are available in French,

German and Spanish. There are two units, covering oral and written communication respectively. They can form an approved National Curriculum short course, equivalent to a half GCSE. They can also provide credit as additional units to a full GNVQ programme. Welsh Language Units are being piloted in some Welsh schools from September 1997.

- *GNVQ Manufacturing Units alongside National Curriculum Design & Technology*. Some schools may offer these units, with opportunities for dual accreditation.

8. BEFORE YOU MAKE UP YOUR MIND

Before you make your final selection, here are a few more questions that might occur to you.

Are all the GCSE subjects recognised by employers, professional bodies, universities and colleges of further education?

The short answer is 'no'. If a minimum number of GCSEs is required by such people, they will sometimes not accept creative and expressive subjects like Art and Music.

The advice is:

CHECK YOUR OPTIONS ARE SUITABLE FOR YOUR LONG-TERM PLANS.

But don't get the idea that subjects like Art and Music are not good courses to take. They are. It depends on what you want to do. For example, if you are thinking of becoming a graphic designer or an architect, then you should take Art. And that is quite apart from the value of such subjects in helping you develop a broader range of personal skills and interests.

Why do employers and colleges often ask for five subjects taken all at one time?

By asking for five subjects at one sitting, employers can expect you to be capable of coping with a lot of sustained work. It gives them a better idea of your all-round ability.

What are 'academic' subjects?

You'll hear people talk about 'academic' subjects. They are referring to subjects that are considered to involve more theoretical work, rather than practical skills.

This distinction is no longer a helpful one, since it creates an artificial divide between the 'academic' subjects and the practical and 'vocational' courses. GCSE has put increasing emphasis on relevance and practical skills, while most of the subjects labelled 'practical' or 'vocational' are intellectually demanding in at least some of their components.

What can I do if the GCSE subject I want to do is not offered at my school?

The best advice is to wait until you are 16, when you'll probably be able to find it at a college, where the range of subjects offered is sometimes wider. In fact, many sixth form teachers and tutors suggest students take an additional GCSE as well as A-levels or other courses they may be taking.

If, however, you want to take the subject before then, you may be able to find a specialist tutor, although this will not always be easy.

Can you get the top grade in all subjects?

Yes, but only if your syllabuses have been designed to include all the work necessary for the top grade or level to be awarded. If it is more appropriate to your needs, the syllabus in some subjects may be designed so that the work involved will earn, at the highest, a grade C. Similarly, it is possible for syllabuses to be designed so that the lowest level that can be awarded for the work involved is a grade E: see the paragraphs on tiering in Chapter 5.

Your teacher would tell you if a course you will be doing involves all the work required for the top-level awards or if it is restricted in some way.

It is also important to remember that if you opt for an exam on high-level papers with, say, grade C as the lowest level available, you are NOT guaranteed that minimum. If you fail to achieve that minimum standard, you will be UNGRADED. In 1996, approximately 5% of candidates entered for the higher tier did not score sufficient marks to reach the minimum standard for grade D and were therefore unclassified.

Why do I have to start selecting my GCSE subjects so early in Year 9 (Year 10 in Northern Ireland)?

A large school might well have over 200 students in one year, choosing from quite a few different subjects. Drawing up a timetable to suit everyone, including the students and the teachers, is a major task. These days most schools make at least some use of a computer, but it still takes time.

9. CHOOSING THE RIGHT GCSEs FOR YOUR CAREER

This guide will tell you the GCSEs you should consider studying if you have a certain career, or possibly several careers, in mind.

There are different ways of getting into many careers – but the usual method for most careers, and the ONLY way for many, is through a RECOGNISED TRAINING COURSE OR A DEGREE, PROFESSIONAL OR OTHER COURSE.

There are other less rigid forms of entry to some careers. You will always hear about people who have succeeded in different walks of life without qualifications. But they are the exceptions. For the vast majority of us the only way is through qualifications.

To check the qualifications you will need, this is what you do:

- Look up all the careers that interest you.
- Write down all the GCSE subjects required.
- Make a list of all the different subjects mentioned.

This will give you a good base on which to build your choice of subject. You should do further research in your school careers library and/or in your local careers office library. The books and leaflets there will probably be filed under the Careers Library Classification Index (CLCI). We have included the CLCI reference for each job in our listings, but your careers teacher or careers adviser will give you any help you need in finding your way around the library. Other booklets and leaflets that may help you to find out more about careers and courses at this stage include:

Job Outlines
Signposts box
'Occupations'
'Working in...' series
Directory of Further Education

Don't forget the range of computer programs that help you look at your interests and abilities and which produce a list of possible jobs linked to those interests and abilities. You may already have tried one of these programs, but if not, ask if they are available in your school or at the local careers office.

The information given for each occupation is as follows.

NAME OF JOB

Entry levels = the points at which entry is possible for school/college leavers. The codes used are:

N = No qualifications necessary.
G = GCSEs (or S Grades) expected, but no specific grades.
G+ = GCSEs at grades A–C (or S Grades 1–3)
GD = Full-time diploma or other training course which is entered after GCSEs (or S Grades), eg BTEC National Diploma.
A = One or more A-levels.
AD = Full-time diploma or degree which is entered after A-levels or National Diploma, eg BTEC Higher National Diploma or BA/BSc degree.

GCSEs normally required = Numbers required or any specific subjects required or preferred.
GCSEs which may be useful = These are subjects which you may wish to consider taking as they can be helpful, but are not essential.
Other academic /training requirements = Full-time study beyond GCSE level which is needed before entering the career – eg A-levels, secretarial course, BTEC National Diploma, degree, etc.
Personality/physical requirements = Any special considerations in addition to academic qualifications.

What is a 'good spread' of GCSEs?

A good spread of GCSEs usually means five or more subjects, all at grade C or above (or S Grades at 3 or above in Scotland).

Although we mentioned Scottish equivalents (eg S Grades and SQA), the position in Scotland is substantially different. For example, the Scottish Higher system is different from A-levels in England

and Wales, while there are also different career structures for some professions in Scotland. As a consequence, Scottish readers (or those anticipating a career in Scotland) are advised to seek more detailed information, where it seems appropriate.

I'M THINKING ABOUT A LEGAL CAREER

BARRISTER — LAB 1

Entry levels: AD.

GCSEs normally required: usually 5 GCSEs at grade C or above. English required.

GCSEs which may be useful: history, modern languages.

Other academic/training requirements: degree is essential, some advantage in a law degree – selectors at certain law schools may prefer arts/social science A-levels. For those wishing to practise in Scotland, a law degree should be taken at a Scottish university.

Personality/physical requirements: communication skills; analytical ability; ability to argue a case; logic and clear-thinking capabilities; a good voice is advantageous.

BARRISTER'S CLERK — LAZ 1

Entry levels: G+, A, AD.

GCSEs normally required: 4 at grade C or above, including English and Mathematics.

GCSEs which may be useful: IT.

Other academic/training requirements: none before entry.

Personality/physical requirements: ability to organise, discretion.

LEGAL EXECUTIVE — LAD 1

Entry levels: G+, A.

GCSEs normally required: 4 at grade C or above. English required, other subjects must be academic – technical and craft subjects are not accepted.

GCSEs which may be useful: business studies.

Other academic/training requirements: A-levels (or equivalent) sometimes preferred.

Personality/physical requirements: organising ability; logic.

LEGAL SECRETARY LAZ 2

Entry levels: G+, GD, A.

GCSEs normally required: generally 3 or 4 at grade C or above, including English.

GCSEs which may be useful: business studies, IT.

Other academic/training requirements: secretarial course; A-levels may be advantageous.

Personality/physical requirements: pleasant manner; ability to organise; discretion.

SOLICITOR LAC 1

Entry levels: AD.

GCSEs normally required: 5 GCSEs at grade C or above. English required.

GCSEs which may be useful: modern languages, history.

Other academic/training requirements: entry after A-level is no longer possible. Some advantage in taking a law degree – selectors at certain schools prefer arts/social science A-levels (in Scotland H grade in English, plus maths or a science or a foreign language).

Personality/physical requirements: communication skills; ability to argue a case; clear thinking.

See also: 'I'm thinking about a career in security'.

I'M THINKING ABOUT A CAREER IN THE GREAT OUTDOORS

FARM MANAGER WAB 3

Entry levels: GD, AD.

GCSEs normally required: 4 GCSEs at grade C or above, to include English and 2 maths/science subjects.

GCSEs which may be useful: business studies.

Other academic/training requirements: diploma entered after GCSEs or A-levels (including a science); or degree. Practical experience required before diploma/degree in each case.

Personality/physical requirements: fitness, organising ability; business sense; scientific interest.

FARMWORKER — WAB 1

Entry levels: N, G.

GCSEs normally required: none specified, but GCSEs may help.

GCSEs which may be useful: English, maths, science, practical subjects.

Other academic/training requirements: none before entry.

Personality/physical requirements: fitness; strength; ability to endure bad weather and to work with little supervision; sense of responsibility; mechanical aptitude; good with animals.

FISH FARMER — WAG 3

Entry levels: G+, GD, AD.

GCSEs normally required: 4 or more GCSEs at grade C or above. Double science (or equivalent) preferred.

Other academic/training requirements: diplomas are now available after GCSEs or science A-levels; science-based degrees also offered.

Personality/physical requirements: fitness; organising ability.

FISHERMAN — WAH 1

Entry levels: N, G.

GCSEs normally required: no special requirements.

GCSEs which may be useful: nautical studies, geography.

Other academic/training requirements: none before entry.

Personality/physical requirements: physical fitness and strength; courage; ability to endure harsh weather; good at teamwork.

FOREST OFFICER — WAF 1

Entry levels: GD, AD.

GCSEs normally required: 4 GCSEs at grade C or above, to include English, maths and science.

GCSEs which may be useful: environmental science, geography.

Other academic/training requirements: diploma entered after GCSEs and practical experience; or forestry degree (needs science A-levels). Practical experience helpful before entry into some training routes.

Personality/physical requirements: fitness; organising ability; business sense for commercial forestry.

FOREST WORKER — WAF 1

Entry levels: N, G.

GCSEs normally required: none specified but GCSEs helpful because of competition for jobs.

GCSEs which may be useful: science, practical subjects.

Other academic/training requirements: none before entry.

Personality/physical requirements: fitness; strength; ability to endure bad weather; care in handling plants; safety awareness; mechanical aptitude; ability to work alone and unsupervised.

GAMEKEEPER — WAM 4

Entry levels: N, G.

GCSEs normally required: no formal qualifications needed but GCSEs may help because of competition.

GCSEs which may be useful: sciences (particularly for biology, rural science, environmental science content), practical subjects.

Other academic/training requirements: none before entry.

Personality/physical requirements: fitness; ability to work alone and unsupervised; sense of responsibility; carefulness in handling young birds etc; willingness to learn to drive and shoot; versatility.

GARDENER — WAD 1

Entry levels: N, G.

GCSEs normally required: none specified.

GCSEs which may be useful: sciences (particularly for biology, rural science, environmental science content).

Other academic/training requirements: none before entry.

Personality/physical requirements: reasonable fitness; tidy workmanship; care in handling plants; eye for design and colour; ability to work with little supervision and alone.

HORTICULTURAL MANAGER — WAD 1/WAB 9

Entry levels: GD, AD.

GCSEs normally required: 4 or more at grade C or above, to include English (or English subject) and 2 maths or science subjects.

GCSEs which may be useful: business studies, geography.

Other academic/training requirements: either National Diploma after GCSEs; or Higher National Diploma or degree after A-levels (including a science).

Personality/physical requirements: reasonable fitness; organising ability; business sense for commercial horticulture; eye for design/colour for amenity horticulture; scientific interest.

HORTICULTURAL WORKER WAD 1

Entry levels: N, G, G+.

GCSEs normally required: some preference for people with GCSEs, especially in science subjects.

Other academic/training requirements: none before entry.

Personality/physical requirements: fitness and stamina; mechanical aptitude to deal with motorised equipment; care in handling plants and crops.

LANDSCAPE ARCHITECT UL 1

Entry levels: AD.

GCSEs normally required: 5 GCSEs at grade C or above, including English, maths or science, and either history or geography or a foreign language.

GCSEs which may be useful: art, biology, botany, design and technology, environmental science, geology.

Other academic/training requirements: diploma or degree in landscape architecture, for which A-levels (eg in subjects mentioned above) are needed.

Personality/physical requirements: creative or design ability; good communication skills; practical but imaginative outlook; interest in environment.

PARK KEEPER/GROUNDS STAFF WAD 1

Entry levels: N, G.

GCSEs normally required: none specified but they may help, of course.

GCSEs which may be useful: sciences.

Other academic/training requirements: none before entry.

Personality/physical requirements: ability to work alone and unsupervised; ability to put up with bad weather; tidy workmanship.

See also: 'I'm thinking about a career in science' – for Agricultural and Horticultural Scientist and for Environmental Scientist/Ecologist.

I'M THINKING ABOUT A CAREER WORKING WITH ANIMALS

BLACKSMITH SAW 2

Entry levels: N, G.

GCSEs normally required: good general education but no special requirements.

GCSEs which may be useful: maths, design and technology, engineering, science, practical subjects.

Other academic/training requirements: none before entry.

Personality/physical requirements: interest in horses; strength and fitness; manual dexterity; patience.

GROOM/STABLEHAND WAM 2

Entry levels: N, G, G+.

GCSEs normally required: no set qualifications but if you have some GCSEs, you may take equestrian exams.

GCSEs which may be useful: sciences (particularly for biology, zoology content).

Other academic/training requirements: none before entry.

Personality/physical requirements: fitness and energy; real love of horses.

HORSE RIDING INSTRUCTOR WAM 2

Entry levels: N, G, G+.

GCSEs normally required: for qualified instructor, 4 GCSEs at grade C or above, including English.

GCSEs which may be useful: sciences (particularly for biology, zoology content).

Other academic/training requirements: none before entry.

Personality/physical requirements: good at handling people, especially children; patience; real love of horses; fitness.

KENNEL WORKER WAM 8

Entry levels: N, G.

GCSEs normally required: GCSEs are an advantage.

GCSEs which may be useful: sciences (particularly for biology, zoology content).

Other academic/training requirements: none before entry.

Personality/physical requirements: fitness and energy; good observation skills; genuine love of dogs; sense of responsibility.

VETERINARY NURSE WAL 2

Entry levels: G, G+.

GCSEs normally required: to qualify for the Royal College of Veterinary Surgeons (RCVS) Veterinary Nursing Scheme, 4 GCSEs at grade C or above, to include English language, and maths or science.

GCSEs which may be useful: biology, zoology.

Other academic/training requirements: genuine caring for animals, without sentimentality; lack of squeamishness; sense of responsibility; good with owners as well as animals. Applicants for the RCVS Scheme must have at least promise of paid employment at an approved training centre.

VETERINARY SURGEON WAL 1

Entry levels: AD.

GCSEs normally required: good spread of GCSEs, at least at grade C. Entry is very competitive and high academic qualifications are needed. Subjects – English, maths, double science (or equivalent).

Other academic/training requirements: veterinary degree is essential – this requires very good science A-levels.

Personality/physical requirements: scientific interest; manual dexterity; good observational skills; fitness and energy; caring but unsentimental approach to animals.

ZOOKEEPER WAM 7

Entry levels: N, G, G+.

GCSEs normally required: no set qualification but this is a competitive area, and GCSEs may help you to get a job and, later, promotion.

GCSEs which may be useful: English, maths, science, geography, a foreign language, practical subjects.

Other academic/training requirements: none before entry.

Personality/physical requirements: fitness and energy; good observation skills; sense of responsibility; true interest in animals.

See also: 'I'm thinking about a career in the great outdoors' – for farming careers.

I'M THINKING ABOUT A CAREER IN TRANSPORT OR TRAVEL

AIR CABIN CREW — YAB 2

Entry levels: G+, A.

GCSEs normally required: preferably several GCSEs at grade C or above. Preferred subjects are modern languages, English, maths.

GCSEs which may be useful: geography, home economics/food studies, childcare.

Other academic/training requirements: experience in a job dealing with people – eg nursing, care work, catering. A-levels can be advantageous.

Personality/physical requirements: minimum height of about 1.57–1.62m and weight in proportion to height; normal colour vision and, usually, good eyesight. Normally ability to swim required. Good appearance; calm, pleasant manner; clear speaking voice. Minimum age of 19.

DRIVER (Bus, Taxi, Lorry etc) — YAD 1

Entry levels: N, G.

GCSEs normally required: no special requirements normally.

GCSEs which may be useful: motor vehicle studies.

Other academic/training requirements: you'll need at least a car driving licence pre-entry.

Personality/physical requirements: good health and character; some mechanical aptitude can be an advantage; good concentration; good manner with people, if you work with the public.

MERCHANT NAVY DECK OFFICER — YAL 1

Entry levels: G+, A, AD.

GCSEs normally required: minimum of 4 GCSEs at grade C or above, to include maths, science and a subject involving the use of English

GCSEs which may be useful: nautical studies, design and technology, geography.

Other academic/training requirements: entry possible after GCSEs, maths/science A-levels or suitable degree.

Personality/physical requirements: very good health, fitness and vision (including colour); strong sense of responsibility; qualities of leadership; mathematical and scientific abilities; ability to mix well with shipmates and endure long voyages in the same company.

MERCHANT NAVY DECK/CATERING RATING — YAL 2

Entry levels: G.

GCSEs normally required: a minimum of 3 GCSEs or equivalent, in maths, science and a subject showing the use of English.

GCSEs which may be useful: nautical studies, home economics/food studies for catering trainees.

Other academic/training requirements: none before entry.

Personality/physical requirements: fitness; good vision for deck ratings; safety consciousness and sense of responsibility; practical/mechanical skills. Ability to get on well with shipmates at work and socially.

MERCHANT NAVY ENGINEERING OFFICER — YAL 1

Entry levels: G+, A, AD.

GCSEs normally required: 4 GCSEs at grade C or above, including maths, science and a subject involving the use of English.

GCSEs which may be useful: nautical studies, design and technology.

Other academic/training requirements: entry is possible after GCSEs, or after A-levels (preferably maths and physics) or suitable degree.

Personality/physical requirements: mechanical and scientific abilities; good at teamwork; ability to cope with possible boredom/monotony of life at sea; good vision (with glasses if worn) and good colour vision.

RAILWAY FITTER/ELECTRICIAN — YAF 1

Entry levels: G, G+.

GCSEs normally required: GCSEs in English, maths and science are desirable.

GCSEs which may be useful: design and technology, engineering.

Other academic/training requirements: none before entry.

Personality/physical requirements: physical fitness, technical/mechanical abilities.

ROAD TRANSPORT MANAGER — YAD 1

Entry levels: A, AD.

GCSEs normally required: for direct entry at management level – 5 GCSEs at grade C or above, to include English and maths.

GCSEs which may be useful: economics, business studies, IT.

Other academic/training requirements: A-levels and, often, a degree.

Personality/physical requirements: organising ability; business sense.

TRAVEL AGENCY WORK GAX 1

Entry levels: G+, GD, A, AD.

GCSEs normally required: usually about 4 GCSEs at grade C or above. English and maths preferred.

GCSEs which may be useful: modern languages, geography, business studies, IT.

Other academic/training requirements: entry possible at various points – after GCSEs, A-levels or degree, or after suitable diploma/higher diploma course with travel option.

Personality/physical requirements: good organising abilities; business sense; pleasant manner and ability to deal with all sorts of people – calm and diplomatic.

TRAVEL COURIER/RESORT REPRESENTATIVE GAX 1

Entry levels: G, G+, A.

GCSEs normally required: no special qualifications, but good GCSEs are advantageous, as competition for jobs is fierce. Modern languages preferred.

GCSEs which may be useful: English, maths, geography.

Other academic/training requirements: none before entry, although A-levels can be advantageous.

Personality/physical requirements: good organising ability; pleasant and helpful manner with people.

I'M THINKING ABOUT A CAREER IN THE FORCES

ARMY – SOLDIERS AND SERVICE WOMEN BAF 2

Entry levels: N, G, G+.

GCSEs normally required: no special qualifications – but some GCSEs, especially maths, science, design and technology etc, may make it easier to enter certain specialist areas.

GCSEs which may be useful: see above.

Other academic/training requirements: none before entry.

Personality/physical requirements: physical fitness; good attitude to discipline and communal life; safety consciousness.

ARMY OFFICER — B 1/BAF 2

Entry levels: G, A, AD.

GCSEs normally required: depends on the type of commission. Generally, minimum of 5 GCSEs at grade C or above, to include English, maths and science or a foreign language.

GCSEs which may be useful: see above.

Other academic/training requirements: most opportunities require at least 2 A-levels and/or a degree.

Personality/physical requirements: qualities of leadership; fitness; self-confidence and ability to inspire confidence in others; clear thinking and well-organised; liking for communal life; smart appearance.

RAF AIRMAN/AIRWOMAN — BAL 2

Entry levels: N, G, G+.

GCSEs normally required: depends on branch. No special requirements for some trades. Technicians, technician apprentices, air engineer/electronics operators: 2–4 GCSEs at grade C or above, including maths, science and preferably English. Air engineer, air loadmaster and air electronics operator: 3 GCSEs at grade C or above, including English, maths and a science.

GCSEs which may be useful: depends upon branch. Sciences generally useful.

Other academic/training requirements: none before entry.

Personality/physical requirements: fitness; good attitude to discipline; safety consciousness and common sense; practical and technical interests for many trades; liking for teamwork and communal life.

RAF OFFICER — B 1/BAL 2

Entry levels: A, AD.

GCSEs normally required: depends on the branch, but should include English language and maths. Generally, minimum of 5 GCSEs at grade C or above. Science advantageous for many specialises.

GCSEs which may be useful: see above.

Other academic/training requirements: A-levels and/or a higher diploma/degree.

Personality/physical requirements: fitness, qualities of leadership; self-confidence and ability to inspire confidence in others; good organisational abilities; liking for communal life; smart appearance.

ROYAL MARINES – OTHER RANKS — BAB 2

Entry levels: N, G, G+.

GCSEs normally required: none. Selection test involves reasoning, English language, numeracy and mechanical comprehension.

GCSEs which may be useful: see above.

Other academic/training requirements: none before entry.

Personality/physical requirements: fitness; good attitude to discipline; good at teamwork; safety consciousness; practical attitude; liking for communal life and able to endure long periods at sea; ability to swim. Musical aptitude in case of musician entry.

ROYAL NAVY RATINGS — BAB 2

Entry levels: N, G, G+.

GCSEs normally required: depends on the specialism. Many require no special qualifications, but technical specialisms require 1, 2 or more GCSEs at grade C or above, to include English, maths and science. Medical technicians require 5 GCSEs.

GCSEs which may be useful: scientific and technical/practical subjects generally.

Other academic/training requirements: none before entry.

Personality/physical requirements: fitness; good attitude to discipline; good at teamwork; safety consciousness; practical attitude; liking for communal life and capable of enduring long periods at sea; ability to swim.

ROYAL NAVY & ROYAL MARINES OFFICER — B 1/BAB 2

Entry levels: G+, A, AD.

GCSEs normally required: 5 GCSEs at grade C or above, including English and maths.

GCSEs which may be useful: science, languages.

Other academic/training requirements: A-levels normally required; graduate entry also available.

Personality/physical requirements: qualities of leadership; fitness; smart appearance; liking for teamwork and communal living.

I'M THINKING ABOUT A CAREER IN ENTERTAINMENT OR PERFORMING

ACTOR/ACTRESS — GAB 1

Entry levels: N, G, G+, GD, A, AD.

GCSEs normally required: no specific requirements – but GCSEs (preferably 5 at grade C or above) required by some drama schools and for all drama degree courses.

GCSEs which may be useful: English literature, drama, music.

Other academic/training requirements: real talent is essential – the profession is overcrowded. A-levels needed for degree courses. Advisable to have a 'second career' to take up while 'resting'.

Personality/physical requirements: stamina; imagination; good speaking voice; persistence. Ability to cope with a difficult lifestyle, often involving travel.

BOX OFFICE STAFF — GAB 2

Entry levels: N, G.

GCSEs normally required: no specific requirements. Maths may be preferred.

GCSEs which may be useful: office skills subjects.

Other academic/training requirements: none before entry.

Personality/physical requirements: ability to deal with members of the public; ability to cope with being very busy; numeracy – to handle money and give change.

CAMERAPERSON/CAMERA OPERATOR (TV) — GAL 1

Entry levels: G+.

GCSEs normally required: no specific requirements, but advantageous to offer at least 3 GCSEs at grade C or above, including English, maths and science (with physics content).

GCSEs which may be useful: technical subjects.

Other academic/training requirements: experience with sound recording equipment and microphones.

Personality/physical requirements: good hearing; technical/practical interests; patience.

DANCER — GAF 1

Entry levels: N, G, G+, GD, A, AD.

GCSEs normally required: no specific requirements – but GCSEs (preferably 5 at grade C or above) preferred by many dance schools and required for dance degree courses.

GCSEs which may be useful: music, drama.

Other academic/training requirements: real talent is essential for either classical or modern dance and training usually begins in childhood. A-levels needed for degree courses.

Personality/physical requirements: fitness, energy and stamina; not too tall if female. Ability to cope with a difficult lifestyle, often including travel.

FASHION/PHOTOGRAPHIC MODEL — OT 1

Entry levels: N, G.

GCSEs normally required: no formal qualifications; some GCSEs an advantage and 3 GCSEs necessary for eg London College of Fashion course.

GCSEs which may be useful: drama.

Other academic/training requirements: none before entry.

Personality/physical requirements: stamina and energy; good height and very slim build; photogenic features; self-confidence; something to make you 'stand out'.

FILM EDITOR (TV) — GAL 3

Entry levels: A, AD.

GCSEs normally required: good spread of GCSEs at grade C or above, to include maths and preferably science.

GCSEs which may be useful: art, drama.

Other academic/training requirements: A-level standard of education is expected and a post-A-level film course would be an advantage.

Personality/physical requirements: serious interest in film.

FLOOR/STAGE MANAGER — GAT 1

Entry levels: G, G+, GD, A, AD.

GCSEs normally required: no particular requirements, but courses in stage management require 5 GCSEs at grade C or above.

GCSEs which may be useful: art, design and technology, drama, English, English literature.

Other academic/training requirements: pre-entry courses are available

(including a wide range of degree courses in related subjects).
Personality/physical requirements: good organising ability; versatility; fitness and energy.

LIGHTING TECHNICIAN (Theatre) GAT 1

Entry levels: G, G+, GD.
GCSEs normally required: good general education – GCSEs at grade C or above, likely to be preferred. Science, maths and design and technology subjects are preferred.
GCSEs which may be useful: art, drama.
Other academic/training requirements: may first train as an electrician. Some full-time theatre lighting courses are available.
Personality/physical requirements: practical/technical skills; genuine interest in theatrical work; reasonable fitness; versatility.

MAKE-UP ARTIST GAL 4/GAT 1

Entry levels: G+, A, AD.
GCSEs normally required: good range of GCSEs at grade C or above. English, art preferred.
GCSEs which may be useful: science, history, drama.
Other academic/training requirements: hairdressing and/or beauty therapy qualifications required before entry. A-level education preferred.
Personality/physical requirements: good skills with people; artistic flair; practical skills; good eyesight and colour vision.

PROFESSIONAL SPORTSPERSON GAG 2

Entry levels: N, G.
GCSEs normally required: no specific requirements – sporting skill is most important aspect.
GCSEs which may be useful: a good spread of GCSEs will be useful for the career you are likely to need to take up in later life.
Other academic/training requirements: you are likely to be 'spotted' before leaving school, in most sports.
Personality/physical requirements: fitness, energy and stamina; willingness to accept discipline of training schedules etc.

SINGER/MUSICIAN GAD 1

Entry levels: N, G, G+, A, AD.
GCSEs normally required: no specific requirements, especially for popular

music, but for courses in classical music, a good spread of GCSEs at grade C or above, is usually required.

GCSEs which may be useful: music, drama.

Other academic/training requirements: none for popular music. Usually music college training for classical singing – A-levels (including music) may be preferred.

Personality/physical requirements: stamina and energy; ability to cope with a difficult lifestyle, often involving travel. Persistence – this is a competitive area of work.

SOUND TECHNICIAN/OPERATOR (Film/TV) GAL 3/RAL 8

Entry levels: G+, GD, AD

GCSEs normally required: at least 3 GCSEs at grade C or above, to include English language, maths and science.

GCSEs which may be useful: technical subjects.

Other academic/training requirements: a relevant BTEC certificate or diploma at National or Higher level or a BA music tonmeister qualification – either necessary or desirable, dependent on entry scheme. Experience with sound recording equipment and microphones.

Personality/physical requirements: good hearing; technical/practical interests; patience.

SPORTS/LEISURE CENTRE MANAGER GAJ 1

Entry levels: G+, GD, A, AD.

GCSEs normally required: usually about 5 GCSEs at grade C or above, preferably including English and maths.

GCSEs which may be useful: science; business studies.

Other academic/training requirements: although entry with GCSEs is possible, jobs go increasingly to people with a recognised qualification in recreational management, eg at BTEC national or degree level.

Personality/physical requirements: good organisational abilities; interest/ability in sport; willingness to work unsocial hours.

STAGE DESIGNER ET

Entry levels: AD.

GCSEs normally required: good spread of GCSEs at grade C or above; art and design subjects expected.

GCSEs which may be useful: drama.

Other academic/training requirements: course in theatre/stage design, taken either after A-levels or a basic art training.

Personality/physical requirements: real interest in the theatre; strong visual imagination.

STUDIO MANAGER (Radio) GAL 2

Entry levels: AD.

GCSEs normally required: good spread of GCSEs, preferably including English and science.

GCSEs which may be useful: practical subjects.

Other academic/training requirements: preference for candidates with experience in sound recording or radio (eg local, hospital or campus radio).

Personality/physical requirements: organised approach to work. Reasonable technical aptitudes.

I'M THINKING ABOUT A CAREER IN SECURITY

FIRE FIGHTER/FIRE OFFICER MAF 1

Entry levels: N, G, G+.

GCSEs normally required: no formal requirements, but some GCSEs preferred, especially English, maths and science.

GCSEs which may be useful: practical subjects.

Other academic/training requirements: none before entry.

Personality/physical requirements: minimum age 18; physical fitness and strength; minimum height 1.68m. Good eyesight without glasses and good colour vision; good hearing and balance. Courage and safety consciousness; good teamwork; willingness to work shifts.

POLICE OFFICER MAB 1

Entry levels: N, G, G+, A, D.

GCSEs normally required: no specific requirements, but 4 GCSEs at grade C or above, including English and maths, may exempt you from the standard entry test.

GCSEs which may be useful: social sciences.

Other academic/training requirements: some entrants have A-levels or a degree.

Personality/physical requirements: minimum age 18.5 (16 for cadets, where available). Minimum height requirements are tending to disappear.

Character, health, eyesight and physique must be good. Qualities of leadership; ability to work in a team and accept discipline; willingness to work shifts.

PRISON GOVERNOR — MAD 1

Entry levels: AD.

GCSEs normally required: good spread of GCSEs at grade C or above, including English.

GCSEs which may be useful: social sciences.

Other academic/training requirements: usually A-levels and a degree (subjects like social sciences or psychology are useful).

Personality/physical requirements: physical fitness, qualities of leadership; understanding of people; good health; stable personality.

PRISON OFFICER — MAD 1

Entry levels: N, G, G+.

GCSEs normally required: no formal entrance requirements. English preferred. Applicants take aptitude test.

GCSEs which may be useful: social sciences.

Other academic/training requirements: none before entry.

Personality/physical requirements: minimum age 20. Minimum height generally 1.67m for men and 1.60m for women. Stable personality; ability to deal authoritatively but sensitively with people; good health and physique; liking for teamwork and discipline.

I'M THINKING ABOUT A CAREER IN HOME ECONOMICS OR THE HOTEL AND CATERING INDUSTRY

CHEF/COOK — IC 1

Entry levels: N, G, GD.

GCSEs normally required: no specific requirements, but some GCSEs are usually an advantage, especially for college courses.

GCSEs which may be useful: home economics/food studies, science, French.

Other academic/training requirements: either direct entry at 16 (perhaps via Youth Training) or full-time college course first.

Personality/physical requirements: calm approach to pressure; ability to withstand hot working conditions; very high standards of hygiene; flair and imagination; good organising abilities and qualities of leadership, if aiming to be a chef in a big kitchen.

DOMESTIC STAFF IB 1/IC 4

Entry levels: N, G.

GCSEs normally required: no formal qualifications needed.

GCSEs which may be useful: home economics/food studies.

Other academic/training requirements: none before entry.

Personality/physical requirements: fitness and energy; tidy worker; liking for making things look nice. Often, willing to work unsocial hours.

FAST FOOD SHOP MANAGER IC 2

Entry levels: G+, GD, A, AD.

GCSEs normally required: about 4 GCSEs at grade C or above, subjects preferably to include English and maths.

GCSEs which may be useful: home economics/food studies, business studies.

Other academic/training requirements: perhaps a business studies or catering course, after GCSEs or A-levels; some graduate entry.

Personality/physical requirements: good organisational abilities and staff management skills. Interest in selling.

HOME ECONOMIST ID 1

Entry levels: GD, AD.

GCSEs normally required: 3–4 GCSEs at grade C or above, to include English and science.

GCSEs which may be useful: maths, home economics/food studies.

Other academic/training requirements: diploma/higher diploma taken after GCSEs/A-level(s); or a degree (science A-levels preferred).

Personality/physical requirements: good communication skills; self-confidence; sympathetic approach to people and their problems. For research work, a meticulous scientific approach.

HOTEL/CATERING MANAGER IB 2

Entry levels: GD, AD.

GCSEs normally required: 3–4 GCSEs at grade C or above, to include English (or English subject); maths and science preferred.

GCSEs which may be useful: home economics/food studies, business studies, French.
Other academic/training requirements: hotel and catering management diploma/higher diploma either after GCSEs or A-levels; or a degree.
Personality/physical requirements: good organisational abilities and qualities of leadership. A pleasant and helpful manner with customers.

HOTEL/HOUSEKEEPER IC 4

Entry levels: G, G+, GD.
GCSEs normally required: good general education; 4 GCSEs at grade C or above (including English, maths and science) allow you to take higher level training.
GCSEs which may be useful: home economics/food studies, science, art/design, business studies.
Other academic/training requirements: you can start after GCSE and train part-time, or take a full-time course before entering employment.
Personality/physical requirements: good organisational abilities; flair for making things look good; interest in furnishings and interior decoration; strong sense of hygiene and cleanliness.

HOTEL RECEPTIONIST IC 4

Entry levels: G+, GD.
GCSEs normally required: usually at least 2 GCSEs at grade C or above; English and maths preferred.
GCSEs which may be useful: modern languages, business studies, IT/office skills.
Other academic/training requirements: some office training and preferably a specific hotel receptionist course – this can be started after GCSEs.
Personality/physical requirements: pleasant manner with people; smart appearance; good organisational skills; willingness to work shifts.

KITCHEN ASSISTANT IC 1

Entry levels: N, G.
GCSEs normally required: no special requirements.
GCSEs which may be useful: home economics/food studies.
Other academic/training requirements: none before entry.
Personality/physical requirements: ability to work quickly and in a team; ability to work in hot atmosphere and put up with standing a lot; strong sense of hygiene and personal cleanliness; tidy worker.

WAITER/WAITRESS — IC 3

Entry levels: N, G.

GCSEs normally required: no special requirements.

GCSEs which may be useful: home economics/food studies.

Other academic/training requirements: none before entry.

Personality/physical requirements: good appearance. Faultless standard of personal cleanliness. Pleasant manner with customers; ability to work quickly under pressure.

See also: 'I'm thinking about a career in health, medicine and personal services' – for Dietician.

I'M THINKING ABOUT A CAREER IN HEALTH, MEDICINE OR PERSONAL SERVICES

AMBULANCE STAFF — JOC 1

Entry levels: N, G.

GCSEs normally required: for some entry schemes, applicants may need 4 GCSEs, preferably including English, maths and science.

GCSEs which may be useful: see above.

Other academic/training requirements: none before entry, but experience of working with people is usually sought.

Personality/physical requirements: minimum age 18 (16, where cadet schemes operate); fitness and strength; calm and understanding nature; pleasant and helpful manner with patients. Driving licence for ambulance work.

BEAUTICIAN/BEAUTY THERAPIST — IK 1

Entry levels: N, G, G+, GD, AD.

GCSEs normally required: minimum of 3 GCSEs preferred, to include English and preferably science.

GCSEs which may be useful: see above.

Other academic/training requirements: normally a college course after GCSEs or A-levels.

Personality/physical requirements: liking for people and pleasant manner; fitness and stamina; ability to use electrical equipment etc; smart, well-groomed appearance and a high standard of personal hygiene; manual dexterity.

CHIROPODIST — JAT 1

Entry levels: AD.
GCSEs normally required: 5 GCSEs at grade C or above, to include English and double science (or equivalent).
GCSEs which may be useful: see above.
Other academic/training requirements: at least 2 A-levels (sciences preferred) then a full-time training course.
Personality/physical requirements: liking for work with people, especially children and the elderly; manual dexterity and practical skills; care and patience; interest in self-employment if willing to practise privately.

CHIROPRACTOR — JOD 3

Entry levels: AD.
GCSEs normally required: 5 GCSEs at grade C or above, to include English and double science.
GCSEs which may be useful: see above.
Other academic/training requirements: 3 A-levels (sciences), then a full-time training course. Minimum age 18.
Personality/physical requirements: sensitive touch; calm and reassuring manner with patients; fitness and stamina; business sense.

DENTAL HYGIENIST — JAF 4

Entry levels: G+, A.
GCSEs normally required: 5 GCSEs at grade C or above, to include English language and science.
GCSEs which may be useful: see above.
Other academic/training requirements: experience as a dental surgery assistant. Applicants should normally be at least 20.
Personality/physical requirements: pleasant and reassuring manner; good communication skills; manual dexterity; faultless personal hygiene.

DENTAL NURSE — JAF 5

Entry levels: N, G, G+, GD.
GCSEs normally required: no formal entry qualifications, but good general education expected – often 2–4 GCSEs at grade C or above, preferably including English and science.
GCSEs which may be useful: see above.
Other academic/training requirements: none before entry usually, although full-time courses are available in some areas.

Personality/physical requirements: pleasant and helpful manner; high standards of personal hygiene; manual dexterity, physical fitness.

DENTAL TECHNICIAN JAF 2

Entry levels: G, G+.

GCSEs normally required: usually 4 GCSEs at grade C or above, to include English, maths and science. Some scope with 3–4 GCSEs, grades D–E, normally to include English, maths and science.

GCSEs which may be useful: practical/technical subjects.

Other academic/training requirements: can start in employment after GCSEs, or first take a full-time course.

Personality/physical requirements: manual dexterity; precision; technical and scientific aptitude; good colour vision.

DENTIST JAF 3

Entry levels: AD.

GCSEs normally required: good spread of GCSEs at grade C or above, to include maths and double science (or equivalent), English language preferred.

GCSEs which may be useful: see above.

Other academic/training requirements: science A-levels, then dentistry degree.

Personality/physical requirements: manual dexterity; technical and scientific aptitude; good communication skills and reassuring manner with patients; ability to cope with pressure of work. Business sense if planning to enter private practice.

DIETITIAN JAV 1

Entry levels: AD.

GCSEs normally required: minimum of 5 GCSEs at grade C or above, to include English and double science, and preferably maths.

GCSEs which may be useful: home economics/food studies.

Other academic/training requirements: 2 A-levels (chemistry and another science) – or sometimes BTEC/SCOTVEC National Diploma/Certificate in science at a good standard – then a degree (usually dietetics).

Personality/physical requirements: scientific aptitude; good communication skills; ability to relate to all sorts of people; interest in food and nutrition.

DISPENSING OPTICIAN JAL 1

Entry levels: G+, GD.

GCSEs normally required: 5 GCSEs at grade C or above, including English, maths and science.

GCSEs which may be useful: practical subjects.

Other academic/training requirements: you can start work after GCSEs or first take a full-time training course.

Personality/physical requirements: helpful and reassuring manner; good communication skills; interest in selling; fashion consciousness.

DOCTOR JAB 1

Entry levels: AD.

GCSEs normally required: good spread of GCSEs at grade C or above, to include English, maths and double science. High grades needed as entry is very competitive.

GCSEs which may be useful: see above.

Other academic/training requirements: 3 A-levels in maths/science subjects, then a medical degree.

Personality/physical requirements: strong scientific interest; calm and reassuring manner with patients; excellent skills of observation; concentration; willingness to work long, unsocial hours.

HAIRDRESSER IL 1

Entry levels: N, G.

GCSEs normally required: good general education; no specific GCSEs.

GCSEs which may be useful: English, art, maths and science.

Other academic/training requirements: college course, apprenticeship or Youth Training in order to qualify.

Personality/physical requirements: pleasant manner with customers; manual dexterity; eye for shape; interest in fashion; no allergies to chemicals, such as perm lotions, and no skin problems. Suitable appearance; high standards of personal hygiene; stamina and ability to stand all day.

HOSPITAL NURSE JAD 1

Entry levels: G, G+, A, AD.

GCSEs normally required: good general education – preferably 5 GCSEs at grade C or above. English and science preferred.

GCSEs which may be useful: home economics/food studies, childcare.

Other academic/training requirements: higher qualifications, eg A-levels, requested by some schools/colleges. Pre-nursing/pre-healthcare courses exist in many colleges.

Personality/physical requirements: practical nature; common sense; caring and sympathetic approach; energy; sense of responsibility; liking for teamwork; often, willingness to work shifts.

HOSPITAL PORTER, OPERATING DEPARTMENT ASSISTANT — JOZ 3

Entry levels: N, G.

GCSEs normally required: no formal qualifications needed, but many applicants have some GCSEs.

GCSEs which may be useful: English, maths, science.

Other academic/training requirements: none before entry, but experience of working with people is usually sought.

Personality/physical requirements: minimum age 18; fitness and strength; calm and understanding nature; pleasant and helpful manner.

MEDICAL TECHNICAL OFFICER — JOB 1

Entry levels: G+, A, AD.

GCSEs normally required: 4 GCSEs at grade C or above, to include English, maths and double science.

GCSEs which may be useful: see above.

Other academic/training requirements: few openings with GCSEs. Most entrants have A-levels (sciences) or Higher National Diploma/degree taken after A-levels.

Personality/physical requirements: meticulous attention to detail; interest in science; liking for laboratory-based work; patience.

NURSING AUXILIARY — JAD 21

Entry levels: N, G.

GCSEs normally required: no specific requirements, although some health authorities require GCSEs.

GCSEs which may be useful: home economics/food studies, science, childcare.

Other academic/training requirements: none before entry.

Personality/physical requirements: minimum age 17/18. Energy; pleasant and helpful manner with colleagues and patients; common sense and practical outlook.

OCCUPATIONAL THERAPIST JAR 1

Entry levels: AD.

GCSEs normally required: minimum of 5 GCSEs at grade C or above, to include English and science.

GCSEs which may be useful: maths, practical subjects.

Other academic/training requirements: 2 A-levels (sciences preferred) then a full-time degree in occupational therapy.

Personality/physical requirements: fitness; sympathetic and caring approach to patients; practical and imaginative attitude to problem solving; patience and perseverance.

OPTICIAN JAL 1

Entry levels: AD.

GCSEs normally required: minimum of 5 GCSEs at grade C or above, to include English, maths and double science (or equivalent).

GCSEs which may be useful: see above.

Other academic/training requirements: 2 A-levels (maths and science subjects) then degree in optometry/ophthalmics.

Personality/physical requirements: ability to get on well with people and reassure them. Liking for meticulous work; business sense if planning to practise privately.

ORTHOPTIST JAL 2

Entry levels: AD.

GCSEs normally required: minimum of 5 GCSEs at grade C or above, to include English, maths and science.

GCSEs which may be useful: see above.

Other academic/training requirements: 2 A-levels (science preferred) then full-time orthoptics degree.

Personality/physical requirements: ability to relate well to patients, especially young children. Good communication skills; ability to observe accurately and interpret test results; patience.

OSTEOPATH JOD 3

Entry levels: AD.

GCSEs normally required: for most reputable training schools, 5 GCSEs at grade C or above, to include English and double science.

GCSEs which may be useful: see above.

Other academic/training requirements: 2 A-levels (sciences), then a full-time training course. For training at London College of Osteopathic Medicine, candidates need to be qualified doctors.
Personality/physical requirements: sensitive touch; calm and reassuring manner with patients; fitness and stamina; business sense.

PHARMACIST JAG 1

Entry levels: AD.
GCSEs normally required: good spread of GCSEs at grade C or above, to include English, maths and double science.
GCSEs which may be useful: see above.
Other academic/training requirements: science A-levels (to include chemistry), then a pharmacy degree.
Personality/physical requirements: meticulous attention to detail; good organising abilities; good communication skills and helpful manner with customers. Strong sense of responsibility.

PHARMACY TECHNICIAN JAG 2

Entry levels: G+.
GCSEs normally required: 3 or 4 GCSEs at grade C or above, to include English, maths, science.
GCSEs which may be useful: see above.
Other academic/training requirements: none before entry.
Personality/physical requirements: attention to detail; strong sense of responsibility; ability to deal helpfully with customers.

PHYSIOLOGICAL MEASUREMENT TECHNICIAN (eg Cardiology, Audiology) JOB 1

Entry levels: G+, A.
GCSEs normally required: preferably a minimum of 4 GCSEs at grade C or above, to include English, maths and double science.
GCSEs which may be useful: technical/practical subjects.
Other academic/training requirements: 2 science A-levels, or 4 GCSEs including double science (grade C or above) give entry at higher level.
Personality/physical requirements: technical abilities; precision; reassuring manner with patients.

PHYSIOTHERAPIST JAN 1

Entry levels: AD.

GCSEs normally required: minimum of 5 GCSEs at grade C or above, to include English, maths and double science.

GCSEs which may be useful: see above.

Other academic/training requirements: 2 A-levels (should include a science – preferably biology); then full-time degree in physiotherapy.

Personality/physical requirements: fitness and stamina; sensitive touch; sympathetic approach to patients; patience and perseverance.

RADIOGRAPHER JAP 1

Entry levels: AD.

GCSEs normally required: minimum of 5 GCSEs at grade C or above, to include English, maths and double science.

GCSEs which may be useful: see above.

Other academic/training requirements: 2 A-levels (sciences preferred) then full-time degree at School of Radiography.

Personality/physical requirements: reasonable fitness; sympathetic and caring approach to patients; scientific/technical understanding; willingness to work shifts for most opportunities.

SPEECH/LANGUAGE THERAPIST JAS 1

Entry levels: AD.

GCSEs normally required: minimum of 5 GCSEs at grade C or above, to include English.

GCSEs which may be useful: maths, modern languages.

Other academic/training requirements: 2 A-levels (science preferred), then a degree.

Personality/physical requirements: good communication skills; sensitive ear; ability to relate well to patients, especially children and elderly people; patience and perseverance; imagination and enthusiasm.

I'M THINKING ABOUT A CAREER IN OFFICE WORK OR ADMINISTRATION

ADMINISTRATIVE/BUSINESS MANAGEMENT TRAINEE (Health Service, Industry & Commerce) C 1/CAL 1/CAP 2

Entry levels: GD, A, AD.

GCSEs normally required: about 5 or more GCSEs at grade C or above, to include English and maths.

GCSEs which may be useful: modern languages, geography, business studies/economics, science.

Other academic/training requirements: various ways of getting started – business studies course after GCSEs or A-levels, direct entry from A-levels or degree (any subject).

Personality/physical requirements: good organisational and administrative abilities; clear thought processes and ability to analyse and present information; ability to supervise staff; good written and oral communication skills; smart appearance.

BILINGUAL SECRETARY CAT 2

Entry levels: GD, AD.

GCSEs normally required: several GCSEs at grade C or above, to include English and a modern language (2 are preferred).

GCSEs which may be useful: business studies, IT, office skills, geography, maths.

Other academic/training requirements: A-level in at least 1 modern language required for higher level courses; bilingual secretarial course to be taken after GCSEs, A-levels (the usual entry point) or a degree.

Personality/physical requirements: good written and oral communication skills; attention to detail; high standards of accuracy and presentation; smart appearance.

CIVIL SERVICE ADMINISTRATIVE ASSISTANT/OFFICER CAB 1

Entry levels: G+.

GCSEs normally required: 2 GCSEs at grade C or above, to include English, for Assistant level; 5 GCSEs at grade C or above, to include English, for Officer level.

GCSEs which may be useful: maths, social sciences; subjects such as modern languages, history, geography, business studies.

Other academic/training requirements: none before entry.

Personality/physical requirements: good organisational abilities; high standards of accuracy and attention to detail; capable of working under pressure for some jobs; ability to deal with the public.

COMPANY SECRETARY — CAP 1

Entry levels: A, AD.

GCSEs normally required: 5 GCSEs at grade C or above, to include English and preferably maths.

GCSEs which may be useful: business studies/economics.

Other academic/training requirements: 2 A-levels or BTEC/SCOTVEC National Diploma/Certificate, and often a degree.

Personality/physical requirements: very good organisational and administrative abilities; high level of written and oral communication skills; attention to detail; self-confidence.

CLERK/CLERICAL ASSISTANT — CAT 6

Entry levels: G, G+.

GCSEs normally required: good general education; higher grade GCSEs are often sought by employers. English and maths preferred.

GCSEs which may be useful: office skills, IT.

Other academic/training requirements: perhaps an office training course before starting a job.

Personality/physical requirements: well-organised approach to work; accuracy and attention to detail; tidy worker; ability to deal with public/customers in some jobs.

ENVIRONMENTAL HEALTH OFFICER — COP 1

Entry levels: AD.

GCSEs normally required: 5 GCSEs at grade C or above, to include English, maths and double science.

GCSEs which may be useful: practical and technical subjects.

Other academic/training requirements: A-levels (at least 1 science), then a diploma or degree in environmental health.

Personality/physical requirements: good powers of observation and attention to detail; self-confidence and confident manner with people; good written and oral communication skills.

EXECUTIVE OFFICER (Civil Service) CAB 1

Entry levels: A, AD.

GCSEs normally required: about 5 GCSEs at grade C or above, to include English and preferably maths.

GCSEs which may be useful: modern languages, history, geography, business studies.

Other academic/training requirements: normally 2 A-levels (or equivalent). but many recruits are graduates.

Personality/physical requirements: good organisational and administrative abilities; good written and oral communication skills; ability to deal with and supervise people; attention to detail.

HEALTH AND SAFETY INSPECTOR COT 1

Entry levels: AD.

GCSEs normally required: good spread of GCSEs at grade C or above, to include maths. English and science preferred.

GCSEs which may be useful: practical and technical subjects.

Other academic/training requirements: A-levels (often sciences), followed by a degree or Higher National Diploma in a scientific or technological subject.

Personality/physical requirements: practical approach and common sense; safety awareness; technical/mechanical aptitudes; good communication skills, including ability to speak well in public situations; powers of persuasion.

LOCAL AUTHORITY ADMINISTRATOR CAG 1

Entry levels: G+, GD, A, AD.

GCSEs normally required: 3 GCSEs at grade C or above, to include English and preferably maths.

GCSEs which may be useful: business studies, IT.

Other academic/training requirements: various levels of entry. You may be able to start with GCSEs or A-levels, but a diploma or degree taken after GCSEs or A-levels may offer advantages.

Personality/physical requirements: good organisational and administrative abilities; written and oral communication skills; clear thought processes; ability to present information clearly; ability to deal with people and supervise staff.

LOCAL AUTHORITY CLERK — CAG 1

Entry levels: G+.

GCSEs normally required: 3 or more GCSEs at grade C or above, preferably to include English and maths.

GCSEs which may be useful: business studies, IT.

Other academic/training requirements: none before entry.

Personality/physical requirements: attention to detail; accuracy; tidy worker; well-organised approach; good communication skills (written and oral); ability to deal with public in some posts; teamwork.

PERSONNEL OFFICER — CAS 1

Entry levels: A, AD.

GCSEs normally required: 5 GCSEs at grade C or above, to include English and maths.

GCSEs which may be useful: business studies/economics; any academic subjects.

Other academic/training requirements: 2 A-levels and often a degree.

Personality/physical requirements: good organisational and administrative abilities; good interpersonal skills; high standards of written and oral communication skills.

RECEPTIONIST — CAT 12

Entry levels: G, G+, GD.

GCSEs normally required: good general education – higher grade GCSEs are an advantage. English often required.

GCSEs which may be useful: maths, modern languages, office skills, IT.

Other academic/training requirements: an office training course or receptionist course is often an advantage.

Personality/physical requirements: smart appearance and pleasant, helpful manner; ability to deal with awkward visitors and cope under pressure.

SECRETARY/PERSONAL ASSISTANT — CAT 1

Entry levels: N, G, G+, GD, AD.

GCSEs normally required: 4 GCSEs, including English, although it is possible to achieve promotion from lower levels of entry.

GCSEs which may be useful: maths, modern languages, office skills, business studies, IT.

Other academic/training requirements: a secretarial course taken after GCSEs or A-levels. Higher qualifications often lead to better jobs.

Personality/physical requirements: calm and capable manner; accurate and quick worker; good at spelling and grammar; good organisational abilities; smart appearance; versatility.

SPECIALIST SECRETARY (Medical, Legal, Agricultural) — CAL 2/LAZ 2/ CAT 8

Entry levels: GD, AD.

GCSEs normally required: about 4 GCSEs at grade C or above, to include English. Maths preferred.

GCSEs which may be useful: IT, business studies.

Other academic/training requirements: secretarial course (preferably a specialist course) taken after GCSEs or perhaps A-levels.

Personality/physical requirements: interest in area of specialism; high level of secretarial skills and meticulous standards of accuracy and presentation; calm and capable manner; good organisational abilities; versatility; smart appearance.

TAX INSPECTOR — CAB 10

Entry levels: AD.

GCSEs normally required: good spread of GCSEs at grade C or above. English and maths preferred.

GCSEs which may be useful: see above.

Other academic/training requirements: A-levels and degree.

Personality/physical requirements: clear thought processes and powers of analysis; good written and oral communication skills; organisational and administrative abilities; high level of numeracy; self-confidence.

TELEPHONIST — CAT 10

Entry levels: G, G+.

GCSEs normally required: good general education; higher grade GCSEs may be preferred, especially in English.

GCSEs which may be useful: IT, modern languages.

Other academic/training requirements: none before entry essential, but an office training course may be an advantage.

Personality/physical requirements: pleasant speaking voice; calm and helpful manner; ability to cope with pressure and awkward callers; liking for sedentary job.

TRADING STANDARDS OFFICER COP 2

Entry levels: A, AD.

GCSEs normally required: 3 or more GCSEs at grade C or above, to include English, maths and science.

GCSEs which may be useful: business studies, design and technology, home economics/food studies.

Other academic/training requirements: A-levels (sciences may be preferred) or equivalent. Often graduate entry.

Personality/physical requirements: meticulous attention to detail and accuracy; good written and oral communication skills; practical and technical abilities; self-confidence.

TYPIST/WORD PROCESSOR OPERATOR CAT 5

Entry levels: G, G+, GD.

GCSEs normally required: good general education, higher grade GCSEs may be preferred. English and maths preferred.

GCSEs which may be useful: IT, office skills.

Other academic/training requirements: ability to type will normally be expected before starting a job – you could learn to type at school or college.

Personality/physical requirements: accuracy; good spelling and grammar; ability to concentrate and work quickly; confidence with electronic equipment; liking for sedentary job.

I'M THINKING ABOUT A CAREER IN COMPUTING

APPLICATIONS PROGRAMMER CAV 9

Entry levels: G+, GD, A, AD.

GCSEs normally required: about 5 GCSEs at grade C or above, with English, maths and science subjects.

GCSEs which may be useful: IT, electronics/design and technology.

Other academic/training requirements: in most cases, at least 1 A-level and often a diploma or degree following A-levels, but still some openings at lower level for those performing well in aptitude tests.

Personality/physical requirements: meticulous attention to detail; ability to concentrate; clear thought processes; powers of logic and analysis.

COMPUTER SERVICE TECHNICIAN — CAV 9

Entry levels: G+, A, AD

GCSEs normally required: usually 4–5 GCSEs at grade C or above, preferably to include English and maths.

GCSEs which may be useful: IT.

Other academic/training requirements: most entrants have BTEC/SCOTVEC awards at National or Higher National level in eg computer studies, if not a degree.

Personality/physical requirements: ability to concentrate and pay attention to detail; systematic approach, but with ability to work quickly.

MICROELECTRONICS ENGINEER — RAL 4

Entry levels: AD.

GCSEs normally required: good spread of GCSEs at grade C or above, to include English, maths and science.

GCSEs which may be useful: design and technology/engineering subjects, electronics.

Other academic/training requirements: A-levels (maths/physics or computer science), then a degree in electronic engineering or related subject.

Personality/physical requirements: technical/design abilities; logical mind; inventiveness; perseverance and attention to detail.

SYSTEMS ANALYST — CAV 9

Entry levels: AD.

GCSEs normally required: good spread of GCSEs at grade C or above, to include English and maths.

GCSEs which may be useful: business studies, IT.

Other academic/training requirements: A-levels and usually a degree or BTEC/SCOTVEC Higher National award.

Personality/physical requirements: analytical and creative mind; good communication skills (oral and written); ability to relate to people; attention to detail.

SYSTEMS PROGRAMMER/SOFTWARE ENGINEER — CAV 9

Entry levels: A, AD.

GCSEs normally required: good spread of GCSEs at grade C or above, to include English, maths and science.

GCSEs which may be useful: design and technology/engineering subjects, electronics.

Other academic/training requirements: A-levels (including maths or science). Many companies prefer a degree in maths, computer science or electronic engineering. BTEC/SCOTVEC Higher National awards also available.

Personality/physical requirements: technical and mathematical skills; problem-solving abilities; perseverance and attention to detail; ability to work well in a team.

I'M THINKING ABOUT A CAREER IN ENGINEERING

CHARTERED ENGINEER — RAB 2

Entry levels: AD.

GCSEs normally required: 5 GCSEs at grade C or above, to include maths, science and preferably English.

GCSEs which may be useful: design and technology, technical and practical subjects, IT, modern languages.

Other academic/training requirements: maths/science (especially physics) A-levels (or BTEC/SCOTVEC equivalent), degree in engineering.

Personality/physical requirements: creativity and initiative; practical approach to problem solving; logic and analytical abilities; good written and oral communication skills; ability to mix with all sorts of people and supervise staff.

ELECTRICIAN — RAK 2/UF 1

Entry levels: G.

GCSEs normally required: usually a few GCSEs at least at grade E or above, with preferred subjects being maths, science, design and technology, practical and technical subjects.

GCSEs which may be useful: see above.

Other academic/training requirements: none before entry which is usually via an apprenticeship or Youth Training.

Personality/physical requirements: ability to concentrate on details; manual dexterity; good colour vision; for some jobs, ability to deal with public or customers.

ENGINEERING CRAFTSPERSON — RAB 2

Entry levels: G.

GCSEs normally required: reasonable GCSEs (say, grade E or above) in maths, science and English.

GCSEs which may be useful: design and technology, practical and technical subjects.

Other academic/training requirements: entry through apprenticeship or Youth Training.

Personality/physical requirements: manual dexterity – good with hands and machinery; ability to work accurately and with attention to detail; liking for teamwork.

ENGINEERING OPERATIVE RAB 2

Entry levels: N, G.

GCSEs normally required: no formal qualifications, but good general education preferred, especially in English, maths, practical and technical subjects.

GCSEs which may be useful: science.

Other academic/training requirements: none before entry.

Personality/physical requirements: liking for teamwork; good with hands and machinery; ability to concentrate; safety consciousness.

ENGINEERING TECHNICIAN RAB 2

Entry levels: G+, GD.

GCSEs normally required: usually 3–4 GCSEs at grade C or above in subjects such as maths, English, science, design and technology, practical subjects. Some possibility of entry with slightly lower qualifications.

GCSEs which may be useful: see above.

Other academic/training requirements: entry through technician apprenticeship or college course such as BTEC/SCOTVEC National Diploma.

Personality/physical requirements: technical skills; ability to understand engineering theory, drawings etc; manual dexterity; attention to fine detail; good communication skills; initiative.

INCORPORATED ENGINEER RAB 2

Entry levels: AD.

GCSEs normally required: 5 GCSEs at grade C or above, to include English, maths, science.

GCSEs which may be useful: design and technology, technical and practical subjects, IT, modern languages.

Other academic/training requirements: maths/science (especially physics) A-levels (or BTEC/SCOTVEC equivalent), plus BTEC/SCOTVEC Higher National Diploma/part-time Higher National Certificate or degree in engineering.

Personality/physical requirements: creativity and initiative; practical approach to problem solving; logic and analytical abilities; good written and oral communication skills; ability to mix with all sorts of people and supervise staff.

MOTOR MECHANIC — RAE 3/RAE 4

Entry levels: N, G.

GCSEs normally required: GCSEs at grade C or above often asked for, preferred subjects being English, maths and science, practical subjects.

GCSEs which may be useful: see above.

Other academic/training requirements: none before entry, which is usually via an apprenticeship or Youth Training. Some college courses exist.

Personality/physical requirements: skills with hands and machinery; reasonable fitness; sense of responsibility; safety consciousness; attention to detail; careful and tidy worker; liking for teamwork.

SHEET METAL WORKER/PLATER — RON 1

Entry levels: N, G.

GCSEs normally required: GCSEs at grade D or above in at least English, maths and science preferred.

GCSEs which may be useful: technical/practical subjects.

Other academic/training requirements: none before entry.

Personality/physical requirements: reasonable fitness; skills in working with hands and machinery; safety consciousness; careful and tidy worker.

I'M THINKING ABOUT A CAREER WORKING WITH CHILDREN OR YOUNG PEOPLE

CARE ASSISTANT — KEB 6/KEB 9

Entry levels: N, G, G+, GD.

GCSEs normally required: no specific requirements, but a good general education is usually expected – higher grade GCSEs advantageous.

GCSEs which may be useful: childcare, home economics, English, social sciences.

Other academic/training requirements: perhaps a 'care' or social work course, or Youth Training.

Personality/physical requirements: plenty of energy; ability to keep children under control; sympathetic nature; sense of responsibility.

CAREERS OFFICER/ADVISER KED 1

Entry levels: AD.

GCSEs normally required: 5 GCSEs at grade C or above, usually including English.

GCSEs which may be useful: social sciences.

Other academic/training requirements: A-levels and degree, or approved diploma. Experience in other work situations is advantageous.

Personality/physical requirements: real understanding of young people; interest in psychology; good communication skills, especially listening and analysing; ability to relate to all kinds of people; retentive memory.

EDUCATIONAL PSYCHOLOGIST KEL 1

Entry levels: AD.

GCSEs normally required: good spread of GCSEs at grade C or above, to include maths and preferably English.

GCSEs which may be useful: science, social sciences; statistics.

Other academic/training requirements: A-levels, then psychology degree and teaching requirements.

Personality/physical requirements: good powers of observation; analytical mind; good communication and interpersonal skills – ability to inspire children's trust.

NURSERY NURSE KEB 4

Entry levels: GD, A.

GCSEs normally required: usually at least 2–3 GCSEs at grade C or above, preferably to include English.

GCSEs which may be useful: home economics, childcare, music, crafts, science, social sciences.

Other academic/training requirements: NNEB course after GCSEs – or even A-levels.

Personality/physical requirements: cheerful, firm manner; lots of energy and imagination; sense of responsibility; safety awareness; well-organised.

RESIDENTIAL SOCIAL WORKER KEB 1/KEB 6

Entry levels: AD.

GCSEs normally required: 4–5 GCSEs at grade C or above, including English.

GCSEs which may be useful: social sciences.

Other academic/training requirements: diploma in social work, after A-levels or equivalent.

Personality/physical requirements: ability to relate well with a wide range of people; good communication skills; ability to handle stress.

TEACHER FAB 1–18

Entry levels: AD.

GCSEs normally required: minimum of 3 GCSEs at grade C or above, to include English and maths. Other subjects will depend on age range/specialism.

GCSEs which may be useful: see above.

Other academic/training requirements: A-levels, then degree and teacher training, or BEd degree.

Personality/physical requirements: excellent communication skills, especially oral; ability to relate to children and motivate them; good organisational abilities; stamina; self-confidence and patience. Other requirements depend upon age range/specialism.

YOUTH AND COMMUNITY WORKER KEG 1/KEG 3

Entry levels: AD.

GCSEs normally required: 5 GCSEs at grade C or above, usually including English.

GCSEs which may be useful: social sciences.

Other academic/training requirements: usually A-levels, then diploma or degree.

Personality/physical requirements: good organisational abilities; excellent communication and interpersonal skills; ability to motivate young people without over-intruding; firm manner; energy and patience. Specialist skills or interests, eg in sport, can be useful.

See also: 'I'm thinking about a career in the social services' – for Probation Officer, Social Worker etc.

See also: 'I'm thinking about a career in health or medicine' – for Doctor (Paediatrician), Speech Therapist, Orthoptist etc.

I'M THINKING ABOUT A CAREER IN SOCIAL AND COMMUNITY SERVICES

CHARITIES MANAGER/ORGANISER KEM 2

Entry levels: A, AD.

GCSEs normally required: about 5 GCSEs at grade C or above. English is preferred.

GCSEs which may be useful: maths, business studies, social sciences.

Other academic/training requirements: A-levels and often a degree. Perhaps a social work training or similar experience.

Personality/physical requirements: excellent organising abilities; persuasiveness; interest in fundraising; good communication skills – ability to motivate people; drive and energy.

HEALTH VISITOR JAD 14

Entry levels: G+, A, AD.

GCSEs normally required: minimum of 5 GCSEs at grade C or above, preferably to include English, maths and science.

GCSEs which may be useful: home economics/food studies, social sciences, childcare.

Other academic/training requirements: nurse training then health visitor's course. A-levels may be an advantage.

Personality/physical requirements: friendly and approachable manner; good powers of observation; good organisational abilities; strong sense of responsibility; good communication skills (written and oral); often, ability to drive.

PROBATION OFFICER KEB 10

Entry levels: AD.

GCSEs normally required: 5 GCSEs at grade C or above, preferably to include English and maths.

GCSEs which may be useful: social sciences, statistics.

Other academic/training requirements: diploma in social work, after A-levels.

Personality/physical requirements: approachable manner but firm when necessary; good communication and interpersonal skills – ability to get on with all types of people; insight and maturity.

PSYCHOLOGIST/PSYCHOTHERAPY KEL 1

Entry levels: AD.

GCSEs normally required: 5 GCSEs at grade C or above, to include maths and preferably English.

GCSEs which may be useful: science, social sciences, statistics.

Other academic/training requirements: A-levels, then degree.

Personality/physical requirements: strong powers of observation and analysis; ability to inspire trust in others; good communication skills, especially listening; self-confidence; insight and maturity.

RELIGIOUS MINISTRY (Priest, Minister etc) FAM 1

Entry levels: G, G+, A, AD.

GCSEs normally required: requirements vary from one denomination to another and entry without qualifications is possible – usually, however, a good spread of GCSEs at grade C or above is welcomed.

GCSEs which may be useful: English, religious studies, history.

Other academic/training requirements: often A-levels and a degree; theological training.

Personality/physical requirements: commitment and faith are vital; good communication and interpersonal skills; approachable, caring manner; energy and drive; ability to motivate others and inspire confidence.

RESIDENTIAL CARE ASSISTANT (eg Homes for Elderly) KEB 6/KEB 9

Entry levels: N, G, G+, GD.

GCSEs normally required: no specific requirements but good general education preferred. GCSEs at grade C or above can enable you to become qualified.

GCSEs which may be useful: English, home economics, social sciences.

Other academic/training requirements: perhaps a college course in a 'care' subject or pre-social work.

Personality/physical requirements: good organisational abilities; sympathetic and pleasant manner, but capable of being firm when necessary; willingness to work unsocial hours (not necessarily resident).

SOCIAL WORKER KEB 1/KEB 2

Entry levels: AD.

GCSEs normally required: 5 GCSEs at grade C or above, preferably to include English and maths.

GCSEs which may be useful: statistics, social sciences.

Other academic/training requirements: diploma in social work, after A-levels.

Personality/physical requirements: real interest in people combined with ability not to get over-involved in cases; good powers of observation; good communication skills (written and oral); power of persuasion; strong sense of responsibility; maturity.

See also: 'I'm thinking about a career working with children or young people'– for Residential Social Worker, Youth and Community Worker.

I'M THINKING ABOUT A CAREER IN FINANCE

ACCOUNTANT (Chartered, Certified, Management, Public Service) NAB 1

Entry levels: GD, A, AD.

GCSEs normally required: at least 5 GCSEs at grade C or above, to include maths and English.

GCSEs which may be useful: business studies/economics, modern languages.

Other academic/training requirements: entry usually a degree (any subject), but possibly also after A-levels or Advanced GNVQ or equivalent.

Personality/physical requirements: attention to detail; good communication skills (oral and written) and interpersonal skills; sound judgement; ability to present a case; smart appearance; honesty and integrity.

ACCOUNTING TECHNICIAN NAB 1

Entry levels: G, G+.

GCSEs normally required: GCSEs, to include English and maths, an advantage.

GCSEs which may be useful: business studies/economics, IT.

Other academic/training requirements: none before entry.

Personality/physical requirements: attention to detail; ability to concentrate and cope with generally sedentary work; neat worker.

ACTUARY NAJ 1

Entry levels: A, AD.

GCSEs normally required: at least 5 GCSEs at grade C or above, including English and maths.

GCSEs which may be useful: statistics, business studies/economics.

Other academic/training requirements: A-levels (or Advanced GNVQ) including maths and almost always a degree.

Personality/physical requirements: strong mathematical abilities; attention to detail and methodical approach; good communication skills (oral, written, numerical); sound judgement.

BANK/BUILDING SOCIETY/ INSURANCE CLERK — NAD 1/NAF 1/ NAG 1

Entry levels: G, G+.

GCSEs normally required: at least some GCSEs at grade C or above, to include English and preferably maths. In some areas, lower grade GCSEs may be sufficient.

GCSEs which may be useful: modern languages, business studies/economics, IT.

Other academic/training requirements: none before entry.

Personality/physical requirements: good powers of concentration and attention to detail; pleasant and helpful manner when dealing with customers; absolute honesty and discretion; smart appearance.

BANKER/BANK OR BUILDING SOCIETY MANAGER — NAD 1/NAF 1

Entry levels: G+, A, AD.

GCSEs normally required: good spread of GCSEs at grade C or above, to include English and preferably maths.

GCSEs which may be useful: modern languages, business studies/economics, IT.

Other academic/training requirements: entry possible after A-levels (or Advanced GNVQ) or degree (any subject).

Personality/physical requirements: managerial potential – good organisational abilities; honesty and trust; ability to motivate staff and inspire trust in others; good communication/negotiating skills; sound judgement; smart appearance; often, willingness to move to gain promotion.

INSURANCE BROKER/UNDERWRITER — NAG 1

Entry levels: G+, GD, A, AD.

GCSEs normally required: at least 4 GCSEs at grade C or above, to include English and maths.

GCSEs which may be useful: business studies/economics.
Other academic/training requirements: entry possible after GCSEs, BTEC National Diploma, A-levels (or Advanced GNVQ) or degree.
Personality/physical requirements: methodical approach and attention to detail; sound judgement; good communication skills (written and oral); honesty and integrity.

INSURANCE SALESPERSON NAG 1

Entry levels: G+.
GCSEs normally required: about 4 GCSEs at grade C or above, including English and maths.
GCSEs which may be useful: business studies/economics.
Other academic/training requirements: none before entry but there may be minimum age limits.
Personality/physical requirements: easy and confident manner with all kinds of people; honesty, discretion and attention; often, a willingness to work unsocial hours; good organisational abilities; often, ability to drive; smart appearance.

INVESTMENT ANALYST NAL 2

Entry levels: AD.
GCSEs normally required: 5 GCSEs at grade C or above, including English and maths.
GCSEs which may be useful: statistics, business studies/economics.
Other academic/training requirements: usually A-levels (or Advanced GNVQ) and degree (sometimes in specialist area).
Personality/physical requirements: ability to analyse and interpret information; good oral and written communication skills; self-confidence and sound judgement; strong interest in economics.

STOCKBROKER NAL 1

Entry levels: G+, A, AD.
GCSEs normally required: no set qualifications, but normally at least 5 GCSEs at grade C or above, including English and maths.
GCSEs which may be useful: business studies/economics, IT, modern languages, geography, science.
Other academic/training requirements: most entrants have A-levels (or Advanced GNVQ) or a degree (any subject).
Personality/physical requirements: ability to analyse information; ability to

work under considerable pressure; sound judgement and financial sense; good communication and negotiating skills.

I'M THINKING ABOUT A CAREER IN ART AND DESIGN

ART TEACHER FAB 7

Entry levels: AD.

GCSEs normally required: 5 GCSEs at grade C or above, including English, maths and preferably art.

GCSEs which may be useful: design and technology.

Other academic/training requirements: A-levels (or Advanced GNVQ) (possibly followed by Foundation Art course), then BEd or art degree plus postgraduate teacher training.

Personality/physical requirements: real interest in teaching; firm manner when necessary; good organisational abilities and excellent communication skills; energy.

ARTIST E 1

Entry levels: GD, AD.

GCSEs normally required: although talent is the main thing (and it is possible to be an artist without qualifications), most artists do take a formal art training for which 3–5 GCSEs at grade C or above may be needed.

GCSEs which may be useful: art, any craft subjects.

Other academic/training requirements: usually art training started after GCSE or A-levels (or Advanced GNVQ).

Personality/physical requirements: real talent and creativity.

DESIGNER (Graphic, Fashion, Furniture, Interior etc) ED 1/EJ 1/SAJ 3/ET 1

Entry levels: GD, AD.

GCSEs normally required: usually at least 3 and preferably 5 GCSEs at grade C or above. Art portfolio more important than particular subjects.

GCSEs which may be useful: art/design, English, subject appropriate to specialism – eg crafts, textiles/dress etc.

Other academic/training requirements: various courses – eg BTEC Diploma or degree in Art & Design after Foundation Course and/or A-levels (or Advanced GNVQ).

Personality/physical requirements: creativity and imagination; real talent; strong visual sense; practical attitudes; good communication skills; ability to work under pressure; often, business sense.

DISPLAY DRESSER — ET 2

Entry levels: N, G, G+.

GCSEs normally required: no particular GCSEs but this is a competitive job, so a few higher grade GCSEs may help.

GCSEs which may be useful: art, practical/craft subjects.

Other academic/training requirements: none before entry, usually, but perhaps an art or design course.

Personality/physical requirements: reasonable fitness; quick and tidy workmanship; good eye for design and colouring; imagination.

FLORIST — OFM 2

Entry levels: G, G+.

GCSEs normally required: good general education – 3 GCSEs at grade C or above, to include English, maths and science for some routes.

GCSEs which may be useful: science, art/design, practical subjects.

Other academic/training requirements: usually apprenticeship/Youth Training.

Personality/physical requirements: quick, careful worker; artistic/design flair; colour sense and eye for shape; good with people if working with customers.

GRAPHIC DESIGNER/ILLUSTRATOR — ED 1

Entry levels: GD, AD.

GCSEs normally required: 4–5 GCSEs at grade C or above, including English and science. Some entry without formal qualifications.

GCSEs which may be useful: design and technology, art.

Other academic/training requirements: specialist training either after GCSEs or Foundation Course and/or A-levels (or Advanced GNVQ).

Personality/physical requirements: technical aptitude and understanding; meticulous attention to detail; care and precision; draughtsmanship skills rather than creativity.

MUSEUM/ART GALLERY CURATOR FAE 1/FAE 2

Entry levels: AD.

GCSEs normally required: good spread of GCSEs at grade C or above, including English and preferably art and modern languages.

GCSEs which may be useful: classical and/or modern languages, history, design and technology, textiles, science for specialist collections.

Other academic/training requirements: usually a degree (often in a relevant subject, such as fine art or art history), after A-levels (or Advanced GNVQ). Many entrants have postgraduate qualifications or research experience.

Personality/physical requirements: scholarly mind; excellent aesthetic judgement; good organisational abilities and communication skills (oral and written); wide-ranging interests.

PHOTOGRAPHER EV 1

Entry levels: G, G+, A, AD.

GCSEs normally required: no specific requirements, but if you want to train formally, a good general education up to about 4 GCSEs at grade C or above, depending on the course.

GCSEs which may be useful: English, science or maths, art, photography.

Other academic/training requirements: training courses are available after GCSEs or A-levels (or Advanced GNVQ).

Personality/physical requirements: good eyesight and colour vision; imagination; patience and care; aptitude for using technical equipment; good oral communication skills and ability to get on with people.

PRESS PHOTOGRAPHER FAC 2

Entry levels: G+, AD.

GCSEs normally required: 5 GCSEs at grade C or above, preferably including English.

GCSEs which may be useful: art, photography; sciences.

Other academic/training requirements: entry is either after GCSEs or following pre-entry course for holders of 1 A-level. Some older entrants have no formal training.

Personality/physical requirements: care and patience; persistent manner; technical aptitude; ability to persuade people when necessary; fitness and stamina; willingness to work unsocial hours.

I'M THINKING ABOUT A CAREER IN INFORMATION OR IN A CULTURAL PROFESSION

ARCHAEOLOGIST FAH 1

Entry levels: AD.

GCSEs normally required: good spread of GCSEs at grade C or above.

GCSEs which may be useful: English, history, classical languages, science.

Other academic/training requirements: A-levels (or Advanced GNVQ), then a degree.

Personality/physical requirements: precision and attention to detail; patience; scholarly approach, yet imaginative and practical; good organisational abilities and communication skills; manual dexterity and strong observational power.

ARCHIVIST FAG 3

Entry levels: AD.

GCSEs normally required: good spread of GCSEs at grade C or above, to include English.

GCSEs which may be useful: modern and classical languages, history.

Other academic/training requirements: A-levels (or Advanced GNVQ), then a degree.

Personality/physical requirements: attention to detail; patience and care; enquiring mind; good organisational abilities; sound judgement; good communication skills; wide-ranging interests.

AUTHOR FAC 4

Entry levels: N, G, G+, A, AD.

GCSEs normally required: no formal qualifications needed – but most authors are well-qualified academically.

GCSEs which may be useful: English, IT.

Other academic/training requirements: none.

Personality/physical requirements: real talent; drive and persistence; self-discipline and ability to concentrate; imagination and creativity.

INTERPRETER/TRANSLATOR FAL 2

Entry levels: AD.

GCSEs normally required: good spread of GCSEs at grade C or above, to include English, a modern language (preferably 2).

GCSEs which may be useful: most subjects; classical languages.
Other academic/training requirements: language degree.
Personality/physical requirements: real fluency in foreign language (preferably more than 1); excellent communication skills; attention to detail and accuracy; ability to concentrate and work well under considerable pressure; for interpreter, good hearing.

JOURNALIST FAC 1

Entry levels: G+, A, AD.
GCSEs normally required: 5 GCSEs at grade C or above, including English.
GCSEs which may be useful: IT; most other subjects.
Other academic/training requirements: entry after GCSEs, A-levels (or Advanced GNVQ) or pre-entry course or degree (both require A-levels or Advanced GNVQ).
Personality/physical requirements: energy and stamina; curiosity and persistence; accuracy; good communication skills (written, listening); ability to work well under pressure; willingness to work unsocial hours.

LIBRARIAN/INFORMATION OFFICER FAF 1/FAF 9

Entry levels: AD.
GCSEs normally required: good spread of GCSEs at grade C or above, to include English. Maths and modern language preferred.
GCSEs which may be useful: IT. Science for specialist/industrial librarianship.
Other academic/training requirements: A-levels (or Advanced GNVQ) then degree.
Personality/physical requirements: enquiring mind and retentive memory; good communication skills (oral and written); interest in seeking out information; ability to deal with all types of people in a helpful way; good organisational skills; analytical approach to problems.

LIBRARY ASSISTANT/INFORMATION ASSISTANT FAF 1

Entry levels: G+, GD.
GCSEs normally required: 4–5 GCSEs at grade C or above, including English and preferably maths.
GCSEs which may be useful: IT.
Other academic/training requirements: entry either after GCSEs or full-time BTEC National Diploma. Information Assistants commonly require A-levels (or Advanced GNVQ).

Personality/physical requirements: reasonable fitness; communication skills and ability to deal with all sorts of people; enquiring mind and retentive memory; usually, willingness to work shifts and unsocial hours.

MUSEUM ASSISTANT — FAE 1

Entry levels: G+, A.

GCSEs normally required: at least 4 GCSEs at grade C or above, to include English.

GCSEs which may be useful: history, art/design subjects.

Other academic/training requirements: A-levels (or Advanced GNVQ) or even a degree may be advantageous.

Personality/physical requirements: careful and tidy workmanship; helpful manner; ability to construct displays can be useful; versatility.

MUSEUM CONSERVATION TECHNICIAN — FAE 1

Entry levels: G+, A, AD.

GCSEs normally required: at least 2 GCSEs at grade C or above, to include English.

GCSEs which may be useful: science, history; craft subjects.

Other academic/training requirements: A-levels (or Advanced GNVQ) or a degree may be needed, although courses are also available after GCSEs in specialist aspects of conservation.

Personality/physical requirements: accuracy and precision; manual dexterity; patience and good concentration.

PUBLICITY OFFICER/PUBLIC RELATIONS OFFICER — OG 1

Entry levels: AD.

GCSEs normally required: good spread of GCSEs, including English.

GCSEs which may be useful: most subjects.

Other academic/training requirements: A-levels (or Advanced GNVQ) and a degree; perhaps training in journalism.

Personality/physical requirements: excellent communication skills; good organisational abilities; self-confidence; attention to detail and accuracy; creativity; versatility.

PUBLISHER/EDITOR — FAD 1

Entry levels: A, AD.

GCSEs normally required: good spread of GCSEs at grade C or above, including English.

GCSEs which may be useful: maths, design subjects, appropriate subjects for specialist publishing, eg languages, science.

Other academic/training requirements: A-levels (or Advanced GNVQ) and usually diploma or degree. Most entrants are graduates.

Personality/physical requirements: business sense and sound judgement; excellent written and oral communication skills; ability to work well under pressure; creativity; good organisational abilities.

See also: 'I'm thinking about a career in science' – for Information Scientist and Technical Writer.

See also: 'I'm thinking about a career in art and design' – for Museum/Art Gallery Curator.

See also: 'I'm thinking about a career in selling, marketing or advertising' – for Advertising Copywriter.

I'M THINKING ABOUT A CAREER IN SELLING, MARKETING OR ADVERTISING

ADVERTISING ACCOUNT EXECUTIVE — OD 1

Entry levels: A, AD.

GCSEs normally required: good spread of GCSEs at grade C or above, to include English and preferably maths.

GCSEs which may be useful: art/design subjects, social sciences, business studies/economics.

Other academic/training requirements: A-levels (or Advanced GNVQ) and often a degree (any subject).

Personality/physical requirements: self-confidence and good communication skills; diplomacy and good interpersonal skills; energy and self-motivation; good organisational abilities; smart appearance.

ADVERTISING COPYWRITER — OD 1

Entry levels: A, AD.

GCSEs normally required: 5 GCSEs at grade C or above, to include English.

GCSEs which may be useful: art/design subjects, social sciences.

Other academic/training requirements: 2 A-levels (or Advanced GNVQ) and usually a diploma or degree (some specialist courses are available).

Personality/physical requirements: creativity and imagination; ability to work to deadlines and under pressure; flair for using words; liking for teamwork; interest in human behaviour.

ESTATE AGENT/AUCTIONEER UM 2/UM 3

Entry levels: G+, A, AD.

GCSEs normally required: 4–5 GCSEs at grade C or above, to include English and maths.

GCSEs which may be useful: science, business studies/economics.

Other academic/training requirements: entry is possible after GCSEs, A-levels (or Advanced GNVQ) or post-A-level diploma or degree.

Personality/physical requirements: extrovert personality; specialist interest for certain types of auctioneer (eg fine arts); self-confidence; good business sense; good judgement.

MARKET RESEARCH INTERVIEWER OB 1

Entry levels: G, G+.

GCSEs normally required: no specific requirements – some GCSEs at grade C or above may be preferred, especially in English and perhaps maths.

GCSEs which may be useful: see above.

Other academic/training requirements: none before entry.

Personality/physical requirements: pleasant voice and warm manner; ability to get on with all sorts of people; self-confidence; smart appearance; sometimes ability to drive. Preference for applicants aged at least 18.

MARKETING MANAGER OB 2

Entry levels: AD.

GCSEs normally required: 4 GCSEs at grade C or above, to include English and maths.

GCSEs which may be useful: business studies/economics, modern languages, social sciences.

Other academic/training requirements: usually A-levels (or Advanced GNVQ) (or equivalent), then a Higher National Diploma or degree (a business studies/marketing degree may be preferred).

Personality/physical requirements: excellent communication skills (oral, written and negotiating); organisational skills; liking for teamwork; broad interests, including interest in human behaviour.

MARKETING RESEARCH EXECUTIVE OB 1

Entry levels: A, AD.

GCSEs normally required: no formal qualification structure, but usually 5 GCSEs at grade C or above, to include English and maths.

GCSEs which may be useful: business studies/economics, modern languages, science, social sciences, statistics.

Other academic/training requirements: A-levels (or Advanced GNVQ) and often a degree.

Personality/physical requirements: good communication skills (oral and written); clear, logical thought processes and analytical skills; strong interest in handling figures and interpreting statistics; ability to work to deadlines and under pressure.

PURCHASING/BUYING ASSISTANT OP1/OP 2

Entry levels: G+.

GCSEs normally required: usually 4–5 GCSEs at grade C or above, including English and maths.

GCSEs which may be useful: business studies/economics; IT.

Other academic/training requirements: none before entry.

Personality/physical requirements: good organisational abilities and methodical approach; liking for clerical work; ability to handle figures.

PURCHASING OFFICER/BUYER OP1/OP2

Entry levels: G+, GD, A, AD.

GCSEs normally required: usually 4–5 GCSEs at grade C or above, to include English and maths.

GCSEs which may be useful: business studies/economics, IT.

Other academic/training requirements: A-levels (or Advanced GNVQ) and/or a degree or business studies qualification.

Personality/physical requirements: self-confidence and willingness to take responsibility; good organisational abilities and communication skills; smart appearance; ability to get on with suppliers/manufacturers; willingness to travel and work unsocial hours; good business/financial sense.

RETAIL MANAGER OE 2

Entry levels: G+, GD, A, AD.

GCSEs normally required: entry varies, but often a minimum of 4–5 GCSEs at grade C or above, preferably to include English and maths.

GCSEs which may be useful: business studies/economics.

Other academic/training requirements: some companies only recruit applicants with A-levels (or Advanced GNVQ, or BTEC equivalent) or degrees (any subject).

Personality/physical requirements: self-confidence; good organisational abilities; ability to supervise staff; willingness to shoulder responsibility; good manner with customers; smart appearance; willingness to work long and unsocial hours and, often, to move for promotion.

SALES REPRESENTATIVE/MANAGER OM1/OE2

Entry levels: G, G+.

GCSEs normally required: no formal requirements, but good general education is expected and some GCSEs at grade C or above are an advantage. Preferred subjects are English and maths.

GCSEs which may be useful: see above.

Other academic/training requirements: none necessarily before entry but A-levels (or Advanced GNVQ), or even a degree, are required for technical sales work.

Personality/physical requirements: self-confidence; pleasant manner and smart appearance; ability to get on with people and to be persuasive when necessary; usually, ability to drive and minimum age 21.

SHOP ASSISTANT/SHELF FILLER/CASHIER OE4

Entry levels: N, G.

GCSEs normally required: usually no formal requirements, but applicants with some GCSEs at grade E or above, especially in English and maths, may be preferred.

GCSEs which may be useful: see above.

Other academic/training requirements: none before entry.

Personality/physical requirements: pleasant manner and appearance; honesty; high standards of personal hygiene; reasonable numeracy; quick worker; willingness to do repetitive work; often, willingness to work at weekends and/or evenings.

TELEPHONE SALES CLERK OM4

Entry levels: G, G+.

GCSEs normally required: no specific requirements, but applicants with a couple of higher grade GCSEs, especially in English and maths, may be preferred.

GCSEs which may be useful: see above.
Other academic/training requirements: none before entry.
Personality/physical requirements: good voice and telephone manner; ability to be persuasive without putting potential customers off; liking for clerical work and attention to detail; liking for sedentary job and, with some employers, willingness to work unsocial hours. Preference for applicants over 18.
See also: 'I'm thinking about a career in art and design' – for Display Dresser.

I'M THINKING ABOUT A CAREER IN SCIENCE

BIOLOGIST/BIOCHEMIST QOD1/QOD 5

Entry levels: GD, A, AD.
GCSEs normally required: 5 GCSEs at grade C or above, to include English, maths, science.
GCSEs which may be useful: statistics.
Other academic/training requirements: science A-levels (or Advanced GNVQ) or Advanced GNVQ and usually a science degree.
Personality/physical requirements: real scientific interests; attention to detail and accuracy; usually, a liking for teamwork; often, organisational and supervisory abilities.

ENVIRONMENTAL SCIENTIST/ECOLOGIST QOL 3

Entry levels: AD.
GCSEs normally required: good spread of GCSEs at grade C or above, to include English, maths, science.
GCSEs which may be useful: geography, geology.
Other academic/training requirements: science/maths A-levels (or Advanced GNVQ) preferred (sciences are not essential), then a degree.
Personality/physical requirements: genuine interest in the environment; good communication skills; analytical mind; liking for teamwork and outdoor work.

GEOLOGIST/GEOPHYSICIST QOL 2

Entry levels: AD.
GCSEs normally required: good spread of GCSEs at grade C or above, to include English, maths and science.

GCSEs which may be useful: engineering/technology subjects; geology; geography.

Other academic/training requirements: science/maths A-levels (or Advanced GNVQ), then a degree.

Personality/physical requirements: good judgement and ability to accept responsibility; good communications skills and organisational ability; often, willingness to work abroad and/or travel; thoroughness.

INDUSTRIAL CHEMIST/FOOD SCIENTIST/ PHARMACEUTICALS SCIENTIST — SAV 2/ QON 1/SAV 1

Entry levels: GD, A, AD.

GCSEs normally required: 5 GCSEs at grade C or above, to include English, maths and science.

GCSEs which may be useful: modern languages.

Other academic/training requirements: science A-levels (or Advanced GNVQ) or Advanced GNVQ, and very often a science degree.

Personality/physical requirements: real scientific/technological interests; attention to accuracy and detail; good organisational and supervisory abilities; liking for teamwork.

INFORMATION SCIENTIST — FAF 8

Entry levels: AD.

GCSEs normally required: good spread of GCSEs at grade C or above, to include English, maths, science and preferably modern languages.

GCSEs which may be useful: IT.

Other academic/training requirements: A-levels (or Advanced GNVQ), then a degree.

Personality/physical requirements: enquiring, research-oriented mind and liking for solving problems; excellent communication skills (written and oral); interest in information technology; ability to get on well with people. For scientific jobs, scientific interest and qualifications are needed.

LABORATORY TECHNICIAN — QOX 1/JAX 1/FAB 13

Entry levels: G+, GD, A.

GCSEs normally required: 4 GCSEs at grade C or above, to include maths and science.

GCSEs which may be useful: English, IT.

Other academic/training requirements: none before entry, although many entrants do have A-levels (or Advanced GNVQ) (or equivalent), some a Higher National Diploma.

Personality/physical requirements: attention to detail and accuracy; ability to follow precise instructions and record information clearly; ability to use technical equipment.

MATHEMATICIAN/STATISTICIAN QOG 1/QOJ 1

Entry levels: AD.

GCSEs normally required: good spread of GCSEs at grade C or above, to include English and maths.

GCSEs which may be useful: science; business studies/economics; IT.

Other academic/training requirements: maths A-level(s), then a degree.

Personality/physical requirements: thoroughness and attention to detail; real mathematical ability; insight and innovation; clear thought processes and analytical ability; often, a liking for teamwork; communication skills.

METALLURGIST/MATERIALS SCIENTIST QOS 1

Entry levels: AD.

GCSEs normally required: good spread of GCSEs at grade C or above, to include English, maths, science.

GCSEs which may be useful: engineering/technology subjects.

Other academic/training requirements: science/maths A-levels (or Advanced GNVQ), then a degree in metallurgy, materials science or other relevant subject.

Personality/physical requirements: thoroughness and attention to detail; enquiring mind and analytical abilities; liking for teamwork.

METEOROLOGIST QOL 4

Entry levels: AD.

GCSEs normally required: good spread of GCSEs at grade C or above, to include maths, English and science.

GCSEs which may be useful: IT, astronomy.

Other academic/training requirements: science/maths A-levels (or Advanced GNVQ), then a degree (usually physics, maths or meteorology) or, sometimes, a BTEC/SCOTVEC Higher National award.

Personality/physical requirements: attention to detail; good observational abilities; good communication skills (oral and written); liking for teamwork; insight and analytical abilities.

PHYSICIST/ASTRONOMER/ASTROPHYSICIST QOF 1/QOF 3

Entry levels: AD.

GCSEs normally required: good spread of GCSEs at grade C or above, to include maths, English, science.

GCSEs which may be useful: engineering/technology subjects, astronomy, IT.

Other academic/training requirements: science/maths A-levels (or Advanced GNVQ), then a degree.

Personality/physical requirements: strong mathematical and scientific interests and abilities; meticulous attention to accuracy and detail; thoroughness; creativity and innovative approach to solving problems.

TECHNICAL WRITER FAC 3

Entry levels: AD.

GCSEs normally required: a good spread of GCSEs at grade C or above, to include English, maths, science.

GCSEs which may be useful: design and technology, IT.

Other academic/training requirements: A-levels (or Advanced GNVQ) (or equivalent) and usually a degree or a Higher National award in a science/engineering subject.

Personality/physical requirements: excellent communication skills, especially written; great attention to detail; thoroughness; ability to work to deadlines and under pressure.

I'M THINKING ABOUT A CAREER IN CONSTRUCTION AND LAND SERVICES

ARCHITECT UB 1

Entry levels: AD.

GCSEs normally required: good spread of GCSEs at grade C or above, to include English and maths or science, and preferably art.

GCSEs which may be useful: design and technology, social sciences, IT.

Other academic/training requirements: A-levels (or Advanced GNVQ) (or equivalent), then a degree in architecture.

Personality/physical requirements: creativity and design ability; practical; interest in people and their behaviour; good communication skills.

ARCHITECTURAL/SURVEYING TECHNICIAN — UB 1/UM 1

Entry levels: G+, GD, A, AD.

GCSEs normally required: usually 4–5 GCSEs at grade C or above, to include maths, English and science.

GCSEs which may be useful: design and technology, IT.

Other academic/training requirements: entry after GCSEs, A-levels (or Advanced GNVQ) or BTEC/SCOTVEC award courses.

Personality/physical requirements: drawing ability; meticulous and careful worker; ability to work in a team; technical understanding.

BRICKLAYER/CARPENTER/PLUMBER/PLASTERER — UF 1/UF 2/UF 8/UF 3/UF 5

Entry levels: G.

GCSEs normally required: qualifications not essential but a general standard of GCSEs at grade E or above will help. Maths, science, design and technology may be preferred.

GCSEs which may be useful: practical/craft subjects.

Other academic/training requirements: apprenticeship or Youth Training to get started.

Personality/physical requirements: fitness; reasonable strength; ability to work in a team; care and thoroughness; for some jobs, ability to read drawings; common sense and safety consciousness; good practical skills.

BUILDER'S LABOURER — UF 1

Entry levels: N, G.

GCSEs normally required: no specific requirements.

GCSEs which may be useful: practical/craft subjects.

Other academic/training requirements: none before entry.

Personality/physical requirements: minimum age usually 18. Fitness and lots of energy; strength; common sense and safety consciousness; ability to work in poor weather conditions.

BUILDING SURVEYOR/BUILDING CONTROL OFFICER — UM 7/UD 1

Entry levels: G+, GD, AD.

GCSEs normally required: 5 GCSEs at grade C or above, to include maths and English.

GCSEs which may be useful: design and technology.

Other academic/training requirements: entry either after GCSEs and

BTEC/SCOTVEC National Diploma, A-levels (or Advanced GNVQ) or Higher National Diploma/degree.

Personality/physical requirements: practical approach; thoroughness and care; attention to detail; good communication skills; aptitude for problem solving; willingness to take on responsibilities.

BUILDING TECHNICIAN UD 1

Entry levels: G+, GD.

GCSEs normally required: 4 GCSEs at grade C or above, including English, maths, science.

GCSEs which may be useful: design and technology, practical subjects.

Other academic/training requirements: none before entry, although you could take a course such as BTEC/SCOTVEC National Diploma.

Personality/physical requirements: practical abilities; organisational/supervisory abilities; liking for teamwork.

BUILDING TECHNOLOGIST/SITE MANAGER UD 1

Entry levels: AD.

GCSEs normally required: 4–5 GCSEs at grade C or above, to include English, maths and science.

GCSEs which may be useful: design and technology.

Other academic/training requirements: A-levels (or Advanced GNVQ) (preferably science), then Higher National Diploma or degree in building.

Personality/physical requirements: practical approach to problems; good planning and organisational abilities; willingness to accept responsibilities; supervisory skills and ability to get on with all types of people.

CARTOGRAPHER UT 1

Entry levels: AD.

GCSEs normally required: good spread of GCSEs at grade C or above, to include English, maths.

GCSEs which may be useful: geography, science, art/design, IT.

Other academic/training requirements: Higher National Diploma or degree after A-levels (or Advanced GNVQ) (geography or maths preferred).

Personality/physical requirements: careful attention to detail; precision; patience; interest in using computers.

CARTOGRAPHIC DRAUGHTSMAN/WOMAN — UT 1

Entry levels: G+, GD, A.

GCSEs normally required: 2–3 GCSEs at grade C or above, to include subjects from: English, maths, geography, art, design and technology, science, languages.

GCSEs which may be useful: IT.

Other academic/training requirements: entry possible after GCSEs, A-levels (or Advanced GNVQ) or BTEC/SCOTVEC National Diploma.

Personality/physical requirements: meticulous concern for accuracy and precision; patience; design and drawing ability; interest in using computers; normal colour vision.

ELECTRICIAN — RAK 2/UF 1

Entry levels: G, G+.

GCSEs normally required: good general education, preferably with GCSEs (perhaps grade C or above) in English, maths, science.

GCSEs which may be useful: design and technology, practical/craft subjects.

Other academic/training requirements: Youth Training or apprenticeship.

Personality/physical requirements: ability to concentrate on detail; normal colour vision; manual dexterity; safety consciousness.

GLAZIER/ROOFER/TILER/SCAFFOLDER — UF 1/UF 6/UF 7

Entry levels: N, G.

GCSEs normally required: no specific requirements, but some GCSEs may be a help.

GCSEs which may be useful: maths, science, craft/practical subjects.

Other academic/training requirements: perhaps an apprenticeship or Youth Training scheme.

Personality/physical requirements: fitness and energy; usually, ability to stand working at heights; liking for working in a team; practical abilities; common sense and safety consciousness.

PAINTER AND DECORATOR — UF 1/UF 4

Entry levels: N, G.

GCSEs normally required: no special requirements, but some GCSEs at grade E or above may be preferred, especially maths.

GCSEs which may be useful: practical/craft/art subjects.

Other academic/training requirements: Youth Training or apprenticeship.

Personality/physical requirements: careful and tidy worker; good with hands; thoroughness; good eye for colour and normal colour vision; reasonable fitness; ability to climb ladders and work at height.

SURVEYOR UM 1/UM 5/UM 6/UM 7/UM 8

Entry levels: G+, GD, A, AD.

GCSEs normally required: 5 GCSEs at grade C or above, to include English and preferably science.

GCSEs which may be useful: geography, geology, design and technology.

Other academic/training requirements: entry possible after GCSEs, A-levels (or Advanced GNVQ) and often Higher National Diploma or degree.

Personality/physical requirements: reasonable fitness; draughting skills for some branches; attention to detail; smart appearance and good interpersonal skills for some branches.

TOWN PLANNER US 1

Entry levels: AD.

GCSEs normally required: good spread of GCSEs at grade C or above, to include English and maths, plus 1 of: history, geography, a modern language.

GCSEs which may be useful: science, statistics, social sciences.

Other academic/training requirements: A-levels (or Advanced GNVQ; or equivalent), then a degree.

Personality/physical requirements: good communication skills (written and oral); ability to analyse information; liking for teamwork; good organisational abilities.

TOWN PLANNING TECHNICIAN US 1

Entry levels: G+.

GCSEs normally required: 4 GCSEs at grade C or above, to include English (or subject testing use of written English) and maths.

GCSEs which may be useful: geography, history, design and technology, economics, science.

Other academic/training requirements: none before entry, although some entrants have BTEC/SCOTVEC awards.

Personality/physical requirements: liking for teamwork; thoroughness and attention to detail.

See also: 'I'm thinking about a career in selling, marketing or advertising' – for Estate Agent.

See also: 'I'm thinking about a career in the great outdoors' – for Landscape Architect.

I'M THINKING ABOUT A CAREER IN MANUFACTURING INDUSTRY

BAKER SAC 2

Entry levels: N, G, G+, GD.

GCSEs normally required: no set requirements, but GCSEs, especially in English, maths and science, may enable you to take a course in baking.

GCSEs which may be useful: science, maths, home economics.

Other academic/training requirements: BTEC National Diploma course available as one entry route.

Personality/physical requirements: high standards of hygiene; strength and fitness; ability to stand high temperatures; willingness to work unsocial hours.

FACTORY WORKER (Skilled) SAB 2

Entry levels: G.

GCSEs normally required: perhaps 2–3 GCSEs at grade E or above. Preferred subjects may be maths, science, design and technology/practical subjects.

GCSEs which may be useful: see above.

Other academic/training requirements: none before entry.

Personality/physical requirements: able to cope with repetitive work; ability in teamwork; safety consciousness and common sense; practical skills.

FACTORY WORKER (Unskilled or Semi-skilled) SAB 2

Entry levels: N, G.

GCSEs normally required: no special requirements.

GCSEs which may be useful: practical/craft subjects.

Other academic/training requirements: none before entry.

Personality/physical requirements: some jobs have minimum age limit of 18. Patience and ability to cope with repetitive work; good with hands; safety consciousness.

FOUNDRY WORKER — SAM 1

Entry levels: N.

GCSEs normally required: no set requirements.

GCSEs which may be useful: practical/craft subjects; design and technology.

Other academic/training requirements: none before entry.

Personality/physical requirements: fitness and strength; ability to withstand very high temperatures; practical abilities and safety consciousness.

INDUSTRIAL TECHNICIAN (eg Polymers, Brewing, Textiles, Photographic Processing) — S 2/SAN 2/ SSAC 4/ SAG 1/EV 1

Entry levels: G+.

GCSEs normally required: ranging from no formal qualifications to 4–5 GCSEs at grade C or above, usually including maths and science, with English preferred.

GCSEs which may be useful: design and technology/engineering, practical subjects, IT.

Other academic/training requirements: none before entry. BTEC National route available for those with 4 GCSEs.

Personality/physical requirements: practical approach; ability with machinery and technical equipment; supervisory and organisational abilities; liking for teamwork.

INDUSTRIAL TECHNOLOGIST (eg Printing, Textiles, Food, Packaging) — S 2/SAR 1/SAG 1/QON 1/SAP 2

Entry levels: AD.

GCSEs normally required: good spread of GCSEs at grade C or above, to include maths, science and usually English.

GCSEs which may be useful: see above.

Other academic/training requirements: A-levels (or Advanced GNVQ) (sciences/maths), then a Higher National Diploma or degree.

Personality/physical requirements: strong technical/scientific interests and abilities; practical approach; good organisational skills; business sense.

PACKER — SAB 2

Entry levels: N, G.

GCSEs normally required: no formal requirements.

GCSEs which may be useful: practical subjects.

Other academic/training requirements: none before entry.

Personality/physical requirements: practical skills – good with hands; ability to put up with routine, repetitive work; quick and tidy worker.

PRINTING WORKER SAR 1

Entry levels: G, G+.

GCSEs normally required: GCSEs at grade E or above are likely to be preferred, especially in English, maths, science.

GCSEs which may be useful: art, design and technology.

Other academic/training requirements: none before entry.

Personality/physical requirements: dexterity and practical skills; care and accuracy; normal colour vision; liking for using machinery.

PRODUCTION MANAGER ROD 1

Entry levels: A, AD.

GCSEs normally required: 4–5 GCSEs at grade C or above, usually including English, maths and science.

GCSEs which may be useful: engineering/design and technology, IT, business studies/economics.

Other academic/training requirements: A-levels (or Advanced GNVQ) and degree (preference for science/engineering/business subjects).

Personality/physical requirements: organisational and management abilities; sound business sense; practical approach to problems; diplomacy and interpersonal skills; drive and energy.

SEWING MACHINIST/MILLINER SAH 4/SAH 3

Entry levels: N, G.

GCSEs normally required: none in particular.

GCSEs which may be useful: home economics (dress and fabrics).

Other academic/training requirements: none before entry.

Personality/physical requirements: neat and careful worker; ability to work quickly; no objection to repetitive and sedentary work.

WOODWORKING MACHINIST/ FURNITURE MAKER SAJ 2/SAJ 3

Entry levels: N, G.

GCSEs normally required: good general education preferred, with GCSEs in maths and design and technology.

GCSEs which may be useful: practical/craft subjects.

Other academic/training requirements: none before entry, but BTEC and degree routes available for those with necessary qualifications.

Personality/physical requirements: attention to detail and care in using machinery; practical skills; ability to put up with repetitive work.

See also: 'I'm thinking about a career in engineering' and 'I'm thinking about a career in science'.

10. HOW HAS GCSE WORKED IN PRACTICE?

How do GCSE results compare with the old system?

Generally, very favourably. The overall pattern is one of higher standards, although reservations about some aspects of the examination and its assessment procedures have led to some of the changes described in this book.

In 1992 38.3% of Year 11 candidates in England, Wales and Northern Ireland obtained five or more A–C grades. This had risen to 43.5% obtaining A*–C grades by 1995.

How will I get my results?

Each examining group is responsible for publishing the results of its examinations on a jointly agreed date, usually towards the end of August.

The results will be sent to your school or college, which will then forward them to you. Some schools and colleges make arrangements for candidates to collect their results in person (often later on the day of their arrival). Your school or college will always tell you the date you can expect to receive or collect them.

How can I be sure that my grade will be accurate?

Proven inaccuracies have been very few in number, measured against the millions of subject entries. Remember that the system of checking marking and results includes impartial observers and that the checking system is very thorough.

There is an appeals system for GCSE grading. In the first instance, you appeal to your school or college and – if they think a mistake has been made – they will put in an appeal to the examining group on your behalf: it costs about £15 for an exam script to be re-examined, but schools are reimbursed if they win their case.

The Independent Appeals Authority for School Examinations only becomes involved when the examining groups' own procedures have been exhausted – and only hears a handful of appeals each year.

In Scotland, by contrast, anyone can query results, although not everyone can instigate the formal appeal.

But, before even considering the appeals process, remember that your teachers are in a good position to make an accurate assessment of your work. The likelihood of an error in the marking is very low.

Has GCSE really proved suitable for all?

GCSE is open to anyone at school or college, whatever their ability. However, it is commonly held not to have been quite as successful for some less able students. This is because of the high requirement for literacy and the demands of coursework.

It is difficult to provide courses and exams that will suit the whole age group. GCSE has fallen short of genuinely catering for all and attempts have been made to come up with alternative courses and methods of assessment for the less able.

There is a range of courses currently available outside the GCSE, including the following:

ASDAN Youth Award Scheme
City & Guilds Entry Level Awards
Edexcel Initial Certificate of Achievement
LCCI Vocational Access Certificate
MEG Certificate of Achievement
NEAB Certificate of Achievement
Open College Network Entry Level Award
RSA Accreditation for Life and Learning
RSA Initial Awards
WJEC Certificates of Educational Achievement

Your school will be able to tell you whether it is operating any of these alternatives.

What advice can you give me on which level of exam to choose?

In subjects where there is a choice of level, you must first of all listen to the advice of your subject teachers. Try to avoid the temptation of ignoring what they say just because the alternative option holds out the possibility of a higher – or safer – grade. They are probably the best judges of your potential.

What difference has GCSE made to the way my subjects are taught?

Most importantly, it has raised standards of teaching. In the early years of GCSE, Her Majesty's Inspectorate (HMI) visits to schools indicated a significant improvement in the standard of lessons observed.

In particular, the HMIs found that study for the new exam had raised both students' motivation and performance and teaching quality. They stated that 'teachers appear to have become more aware of what [students] are capable of achieving'.

GCSE has led to a marked improvement in oral and written work, and more and better practical and investigative work. It has increased the ability of students to show what they know, understand and can do, especially in their coursework. The additional emphasis given to positive achievement in both coursework and the exams is probably the greatest success of GCSE.

Will GCSE prepare me for study at higher level?

HMIs expressed the view that it is 'sufficient of a challenge to form a sound intellectual basis for students going on to A-level'. GCSE has had a positive impact on the numbers of young people staying on in full-time education in order to take A-levels (or Advanced GNVQ) or equivalent courses.

A-levels (or Advanced GNVQ) themselves have begun to change and are likely to be revised further, partly to reflect the differences in the GCSE syllabuses. In a more positive sense, they should also change in order to take maximum benefit from the new skills being measured by the GCSE.

Remember that you need to do REALLY WELL in a subject at GCSE to consider taking it at A-level. Even a C grade is not a good indicator for A-level success in some subjects. This does NOT mean that you can't take A-levels (or Advanced GNVQ) (or other higher-level courses) of which you have no previous experience, as long as this is not simply an 'escape route' and you do have some evidence of your ability to cope.

11. THE GCSE IN NORTHERN IRELAND

In Northern Ireland, the GCSE is administered by the Northern Ireland Council for the Curriculum, Examinations and Assessment (CCEA). The Council advises the Department of Education for Northern Ireland (DENI) on assessment and examinations generally. GCSE syllabuses and examinations in Northern Ireland comply with the GCSE general and subject criteria, taking into account where necessary the distinctive features of the Northern Ireland common curriculum.

What GCSE subjects are available in Northern Ireland?

Accounting
Additional Mathematics
Art & Design
Biology: Human
Business Studies
Classical Civilisation (Greek and Roman)
Computer Studies
Craft, Design & Technology (Design & Communication)
Craft, Design & Technology (Design & Realisation)
Drama
Economics
English
English Literature
French
Geography
German
Greek
History
Home Economics
Irish (Gaeilge)
Italian
Latin

Mathematics
Motor Vehicle and Road User Studies
Music
Personal & Social Education
Physical Education
Religious Studies
Science: Biology
Science: Chemistry
Science: Double Award (Modular and Non-Modular)
Science: Geology
Science: Physics
Science: Single Award (Modular and Non-Modular)
Social Science
Spanish
Technology (Product and Systems Design)
Textiles

As in England and Wales, new National Curriculum and GCSE requirements have been phased in and are now fully operational.

In Northern Ireland the Key Stage 4 (Years 11 and 12) curriculum consists of six Areas of Study, six educational (cross-curricular) themes and a course of religious education.

What are these Areas of Study?

The six Areas of Study are:

- English
- Mathematics
- Science & Technology
- The Environment & Society
- Creative & Expressive Studies (Physical Education)
- Language Studies

Students who have taken GCSE in either English or Mathematics at the end of Year 11 do not have to follow the Key Stage 4 programme of study. However, they must take another 'cognate' subject, eg English Literature (in the case of English) or Additional Mathematics or Statistics (in the case of Mathematics).

National Curriculum programmes of study define the essential content of each subject and are the basis for planning, teaching, learning and assessment objectives. They operate in most Areas of Study: Physical Education came into line in September 1995 and The Environment & Society courses (including History, Geography, Business Studies and Home Economics) in September 1996. All courses in compulsory subjects which do not have programmes of study now have to be approved by DENI on the advice of CCEA.

In The Environment & Society, the choice is:

- a course from History/Geography/Business Studies/Home Economics
  or
- an approved course in Economics/Politics or modular provision selected from a range of modules to include Law in our Lives, Environmental Education, Information Technology, Health/Sex Education, Economic Awareness, Cultural Heritage, Careers Education.

Language Studies provision now consists of an approved course, eg GCSE or GNVQ unit(s) or GOML (Graded Objective in Modern Languages).

Will I have much choice?

Reduction in the statutory curriculum time is intended to allow schools further flexibility to meet students' needs. For example, this can be used to provide additional time for the compulsory subjects, to offer additional courses from within the Area of Study framework, or to provide additional elements such as Personal & Social Education and Careers Guidance.

What about coursework?

Coursework weightings are also different in Northern Ireland. The maximum allocations for coursework are as follows:

Art & Design	60%
Biology: Human	24%

Business Studies	20%
CDT Design & Communication	45%
CDT Design & Realisation	50%
Classical Civilisation	20%
Economics	20%
English	40%
English Literature	30%
Geography	20%
History	30%
Mathematics	20%
Religious Studies	30%
Science: Biology	24%
Science: Chemistry	24%
Science: Double Award	28%
Science: Physics	24%
Science: Single Award	25%
Social Science	30%
Technology	45%

Do we all sit the same exams?

No. There are again tiering arrangements, but these are different in Northern Ireland.

The tiers of entry for Northern Ireland National Curriculum subjects are:

Mathematics	Tier P	grades D–G
	Tier Q	A*–D
Science (Double/Single Award)	Tier P	D–G
	Tier Q	B–D (B–E for Single Award)
	Tier R	A*–B
English	Tier S	C–G
	Tier T	A*–D

12. ...AND IN SCOTLAND

Is the structure of the secondary curriculum and examinations the same as in the rest of the UK?

No. There are several major differences in the Scottish system. Firstly, students in Scotland begin their secondary schooling when they are about 12 years of age.

The curriculum is divided into three stages, the first two of which are compulsory. In the first two years of secondary school (S1 and S2), students follow a broad and balanced educational programme. Towards the end of S2, they choose the courses they will study in S3 and S4.

Does this mean that there is more choice for 14- and 15-year-olds in Scotland?

Not entirely. In effect, Scotland has a National Curriculum for this age group, since all schools are expected to follow certain guiding principles, as defined by the Scottish Consultative Council on the Curriculum (SCCC – the Scottish equivalent to the National Curriculum Council).

All students have to continue studying English, Mathematics, a modern European language and a Science course at S3 and S4. In addition, schools are asked to ensure that students select additional full or short courses meeting the requirements of eight 'modes' or areas of study:

Language & Communication
Mathematical Studies & Applications
Scientific Studies & Applications
Social and Environmental Studies
Technological Activities & Applications
Creative & Aesthetic Activities
Physical Education
Religious & Moral Education

What sort of school-leaving examinations are there?

At the end of S4 the majority of students take examinations leading to the Scottish Certificate of Education (SCE). The courses taken lead to awards at Standard Grade (S Grade) and to short course awards, recorded on the Scottish Certificate of Education.

Do I have to take exams in all the different modes?

Not as such. The S3 and S4 courses are meant to give each student adequate experience in all the modes, but the S Grade courses are not an exact match to the individual modes. A single course may contribute to several different modes.

Students may cover the entire mode requirement by choosing a Core course. For example, it is possible to meet the Technological Activities and Applications requirement by taking an S Grade course in Computing Studies, Craft & Design, Home Economics, Office & Information Studies or Technological Studies or relevant short courses or appropriate activities from these courses. It is also possible to meet this same mode requirement by taking other courses from a range of elective options.

Are all these options available in all the schools?

No. Larger schools are normally able to offer a wider choice than smaller schools.

National syllabuses also allow schools some flexibility in deciding on course content and on teaching and learning methods. So there may be differences in the teaching of a particular course between one school and another.

How much time will I have to study each subject?

There are recommended minimum and maximum time allocations for each subject, based on the assumption that the syllabuses for English and Mathematics would need five 40-minute periods a week and those for other full courses four periods.

The normal minimum time requirement (in hours) for each of the modes, over the two-year period, is as follows:

Language & Communication	360
Mathematical Studies & Applications	200
Scientific Studies & Applications	160
Social & Environmental Studies	160
Technological Activities & Applications	80
Creative & Aesthetic Activities	80
Physical Education	80
Religious & Moral Education	80

The total of 1200 hours allocated to this core of the eight modes represents approximately 70% of the time available to students throughout S3 and S4.

What happens for the rest of the time?

In the remaining 30% of available class time, schools are able to offer a variety of short or modular courses of varying lengths. The most common format for such courses is that of modules leading to the award of the National Certificate by the Scottish Qualifications Authority (SQA). The SQA modules include a number of courses that serve to complement the curriculum at S3 and S4.

The SQA also provides a limited range of short courses which are certificated on the SCE. These are intended to provide candidates with an extension or enrichment of their curriculum in and after the third year of secondary education. The short courses offered in this way are:

Classical Studies
Creative & Aesthetic Studies
Electronics
European Studies
Geology
Graphic Communication
Health Studies
Nautical Studies
Religious & Moral Education

Statistics
Technological Studies

These short courses which lead to certificated awards are 40-hour units which are internally assessed and externally moderated. Awards are ungraded and are recorded on the same certificate as Standard (or Higher Grade) awards.

Schools can also offer short courses of their own design, which do not lead to national certification.

Are Standard Grade courses and exams the same for all?

Not in all cases. In some areas, such as Mathematics, students follow courses at three levels, to suit different levels of ability. In others, such as English, the course is the same for all, but the skills to be acquired are differentiated to suit the different ability groups.

What is the grading system for the Standard Grade exams?

Standard Grade awards are made in terms of a seven-point numerical scale 1–7, where 1 is the highest award. The attainment levels for grades 1–6 are specified by the Grade Related Criteria (GRC) which are available from the Scottish Qualifications Authority on request. Grade 7 indicates that the course was completed but without evidence of significant attainment.

For most courses, there are three separate examination papers at the end of the two years. They are set for Credit, General and Foundation levels.

Credit papers lead to awards at grade 1 or 2, General papers to awards at grade 3 or 4 and Foundation papers to awards at grade 5 or 6.

Normally, students take examinations covering two pairs of grades, either grades 1–4 or grades 3–6. This is intended to ensure that all students have the best opportunity to gain an award which reflects their real ability and achievement.

A Standard Grade award of grade 3 or better is equivalent to a GCSE award at grade C or better.

What else do I need to know about the assessment system?

It is essentially a performance or criteria related method of assessment. In other words, the award is based on the achievements of the individual people, measured against stated standards, rather than on how that individual's achievement compares with that of other candidates.

In order to achieve a particular grade within a particular level, candidates have to give evidence of achievement in all the basic aspects or 'elements' of the subject. For example, in English, candidates will receive separate assessments for Reading, Writing and Talking as well as an overall grade. A Profile of Performance stating the grade obtained in each element then appears on the Certificate beside the overall award for the course. To continue the example of English, an individual student's award might therefore be reported in this way:

Subject	*Overall Award*	*Profile of Performance*
English	3	Reading 3 Writing 2 Talking 4

How will these separate elements be assessed?

In a variety of different ways. In most courses, candidates will have to demonstrate attainment in oral or practical skills and these skills will usually be assessed internally by the class teacher on the basis of work done during the course.

Other elements, such as Writing in English, will be assessed on the basis of a folio submitted to the SQA, together with a written examination. Others will be assessed through a written examination alone.

In all cases, even where an element is assessed externally, teachers will have submitted estimated grades to the SQA. These can be used to improve the SQA grades in the case of any disagreement.

If an assessment is not available for any element, for whatever reason, no overall grade can be given for the course. The only exception to this is when a candidate is not able to offer an element because of a particular handicap or impairment.

What about the assessment of short courses?

The individual school is responsible for assessing candidates taking short courses, with the SQA moderating school assessments to ensure national standards.

The SCE then records any SQA short courses which have been completed successfully.

What happens at 16+?

There is a further, optional stage of one or two years for students aged 16–18 who wish to stay on at school. At present, over 75% of S4 students return to school for S5.

The range of courses available includes courses leading to the Higher Grade of the SCE and to the Certificate of Sixth Year Studies.

Students who achieve a Credit Level award at S Grade will normally sit the Higher examination in that subject after just one more year of study, ie at about age 17. Students who achieve General will probably require a further two years of study, but it should be noted that not all schools can offer a Higher Grade course spread over a two-year period.

Higher Grades have been going through a period of revision, but this has not affected their place in the Scottish educational system and they continue to provide the route for a significant proportion of students aiming to enter the professions, go to university or into other forms of higher education.

What other courses are available?

Although it is again subject to some changes, the Certificate of Sixth Year Studies (CSYS) remains available for students in their sixth year of secondary education. Candidates for CSYS examinations must have obtained a pass at Higher Grade or equivalent. The CSYS is not required for university entrance but offers a focus for more specialised, people-centred learning. Syllabuses emphasise the need for individual study and most subjects include the submission of a dissertation or project report. The CSYS is awarded in terms of a five-point scale of rankings A–E with A being the highest, or are ungraded. Ungraded results are not certificated.

National Certificate modules are also available for students in S5 and S6 as an alternative or complement to Highers and CSYS.

The SQA is developing further short courses which will often be suitable for study in S5 and S6.

Higher Still

A new system of post-16 education for all young people will be introduced from August 1999. The aim of the 'Higher Still' Development Programme is to bring together Higher Grade courses, CSYS courses, SQA short courses, National Certificate modules, General Scottish Vocational Qualifications (GSVQs) and the National Certificate group awards into a single, coherent post-16 system.

13. LIFE AFTER GCSE – OPTIONS AT 16

My options at 16 – how will they affect my choice of GCSEs?

In another two years you will be facing another decision – one that will shape your future. And the choice will be even greater, but you are laying the foundation of that choice now, by the options you are making in your selection of GCSE subjects.

So, before you make your final selection of GCSEs, think carefully about what you might decide to do later on.

The options at 16 are very wide indeed, but the major ones are as follows.

Getting a job

There's no denying that for some school is just a chore – they can't wait to get out and earn their own living. However, fewer employers are now recruiting at 16. Of those that are, you should certainly be looking more seriously at those who are offering further training, preferably leading to a National Vocational Qualification. You need to think about what GCSEs would be preferred, or required, to start a job at 16.

Going on a training course

You may decide not to stay at school. There are various training options for 16-year-olds. They include:

Youth Training

Job opportunities at 16 are no longer easy to find. Youth Training is a halfway house between work and study. It gives you work experience, training and at least the minimum weekly training allowance. There's no guarantee of a job at the end, but very often it does result in one. And even if you don't land a permanent job, you would have some good experience to offer another employer.

But how does all this affect GCSE decisions? Some Youth Training schemes have GCSE entry qualifications, so you should check that the GCSEs you choose are acceptable for any Youth Training option you may be considering.

The Youth Credits system (sometimes known by another name, such as Training Credits) allows school and college leavers to choose and buy their own career training. It also entitles you to more careers advice and guidance to help you make the most of the opportunities available. It is available to every 16- and 17-year-old leaving school or college in England and Wales. You should note that the government is currently considering changes to the Youth Training system, which means that some of the training programmes and their names will almost certainly change.

Modern Apprenticeships

This is a relatively new approach to training for young people: the first Modern Apprenticeships started in September 1994. Modern Apprenticeships are geared to individual needs and provide training to at least NVQ Level 3 (equivalent to two A-levels).

Vocational courses

Other examination courses you can take include:

City & Guilds	Examinations leading to skilled craft qualifications.
Edexcel	The Edexcel Foundation is the merger of the vocational awarding body BTEC and one of the examining groups, London Examinations. It offers Certificate/Diploma qualifications at First, National and Higher National level.
RSA	Royal Society of Arts examinations, principally covering the range of business and commercial studies.
LCCI	The London Chamber of Commerce and Industry, which offers examinations for office skills and secretarial studies.

Staying on at school

This will often involve taking A-levels or an Advanced GNVQ. Courses at this level are essential if you want to take a degree.

A GNVQ Advanced qualification is broadly equivalent to a couple of A-levels. Entry onto courses is therefore at a similar level to A-levels – most schools and colleges ask for a minimum of four or five GCSEs at grade C or above, or equivalent qualifications. GNVQ Advanced level qualifications meet the general requirements for entry to many degree courses. Successful students are also well placed to apply for a range of jobs with good prospects.

A UCAS survey, 'In their own words', consists of the reflections of former GNVQ students on how well prepared they were for higher education. The overwhelming feeling amongst them was that their GNVQ study gave them a strong advantage over other students when it came to presentations, independent study and use of computers. The practical, project-based nature of GNVQs also means that students are not put off by the requirements of research and planning their own work.

The downside was that these same students found that their examination skills were not always adequate for certain demands of higher education and, for some science and business based degrees, that the science and mathematical units of GNVQs did not always provide enough in-depth knowledge.

Post-16, the vocational areas currently or soon to be available at Advanced (and the other two GNVQ Levels) include:

Art & Design
Business
Construction & the Built Environment
Engineering
Health & Social Care
Hospitality & Catering
Information Technology
Land-based & Environmental Industries
Leisure & Tourism
Manufacturing
Media: Communication & Production
Performing Arts & Entertainment Industries

Retail & Distribution
Science

If taking A-levels, you'll probably opt for two or three subjects. The subjects you have taken at GCSE are bound to influence your choice of A-levels. A-levels are of a high standard and in some subjects it may not be easy to cope with the A-level syllabus unless you have studied the subject on a GCSE course – Languages and Sciences are examples of this. So, ask yourself which A-levels you might want to do before choosing your GCSEs.

Some of the subjects offered at A-level include the learning of specific practical skills. In some schools and colleges you can study Dance, Art or Sports Studies at A-level. And, if you want more variety in your studies, there is also the option of AS-levels.

The AS-level is there to help broaden your course of study. At present, these courses reach the same high standard as A-levels, but cover less ground: two AS-levels are generally seen to be the equivalent of one A-level. If you are thinking about taking AS-levels, consider which GCSEs would be appropriate to give you a good grounding in the subjects you would like to study. You should note that there are proposals to change the nature of AS-levels in the future.

Other options in the sixth form or at college

Many schools and colleges offer Foundation or Intermediate level GNVQ courses for students in Year 12 onwards.

For GNVQ Intermediate courses, students are normally expected to have achieved something like four GCSEs at grades D–G or a Foundation GNVQ (or an NVQ at Level 1).

Entry onto GNVQ Foundation level courses does not require any formal qualifications, although applicants need to show the ability to benefit from the course.

You may find that you are also able to take GCSEs in the sixth form. These are usually two-year courses, but sometimes there is the option of special one-year courses, especially in new subject areas. Coursework will normally be a feature, but the syllabus will be designed to ensure you can carry it out within one year.

14. MAKING THE CHOICE

The National Curriculum has already greatly limited the number of options open to students in Years 10 and 11 (Years 11 and 12 in Northern Ireland). However, if your school continues to operate a system with any element of choice in the subjects to be taken at GCSE, it is important that you should think carefully about your choice. This book should have helped you get all the facts you need. You should now be ready to make your final choice.

Use this checklist to make your selection.

❑ Make a list of all subjects your school is offering.

❑ Tick subjects that are essential for your career.

❑ Tick all the subjects your school insists that you take.

❑ Tick any subjects you enjoy/are good at/want to take.

❑ Tick any of the new subjects being offered that you would like to try or think would be useful.

❑ Check to see if you have at least one subject from each of the major subject groups, ie:

English (and related subjects)
Maths
Modern Foreign Languages
Sciences
Humanities
Creative Subjects (including Technology)

and make sure you have taken advice before leaving out any one group.

❑ Count up the number of subjects you have ticked. If it comes to more than six, check with your teachers how many subjects they think you can cope with.

- ❑ Check the coursework commitment in each subject with your teachers.

- ❑ If there are too many subjects or the coursework commitment is too high, work through this list again, being more selective.

- ❑ Remember that there are other people as well as your subject teachers who you can talk to – your careers teacher, form tutor, year tutor and, of course, your family.

Now, how does it look?

Horrendous?
Horrifying?
Difficult?

Look through the checklist and be even more selective.

or

Hard work?
Interesting?
OK?
Just right?

GO FOR IT!

But what if I do choose the wrong subjects, what can I do?

Don't panic! It happens all the time.

It could be that you will suddenly get a new career idea and will realise you need to be studying something else. If you have chosen wisely in the first place, it is unlikely that many of the subjects you have opted for will be wrong. So, if you are part way through your GCSEs, the answer is to keep on studying and get the best possible grades you can in the subjects you are taking. That will always stand you in good stead. Who knows, you might change your mind yet again.

Then, when you get to the sixth form or move on to a college, you can take the extra subjects you need and, because you will be that much older, you should be able to take them in one year instead of the normal two – that is one of the advantages of the GCSE system.

My GCSE decisions

Subject groups

	English	Maths	Sciences
1	________	________	________
2	________	________	________
3	________	________	________

	Humanities	Creative subjects	Modern foreign languages
1	________	________	________
2	________	________	________
3	________	________	________

OTHER SOURCES OF REFERENCE

Subjects and exams for 14- to 16-year-olds: QCA (available also in Bengali, Chinese, Greek, Gujarati, Hindi, Punjabi, Turkish, Urdu, Vietnamese and in Braille and on cassette). Phone 0181 561 4499.

GCSE Regulations and Criteria: QCA/ACAC

CAREERS INDEX

Alphabetical careers index to Chapter 8 (pages 45–111)